Earth, Water,
Fire, and Air

Earth, Water, Fire, and Air

Essential Ways of Connecting to Spirit

Cait Johnson

Walking Together, Finding the Way®
SKYLIGHT PATHS®
PUBLISHING
Nashville, Tennessee

Earth, Water, Fire, and Air:
Essential Ways of Connecting to Spirit

Library of Congress Cataloging-in-Publication Data
Johnson, Cait.
Earth, water, fire, and air : essential ways of connecting to spirit /
Cait Johnson.
      p.   cm.
Includes bibliographical references.
ISBN 1-893361-65-9
1. Nature—Religious aspects. 2. Spirit. 3. Spiritual life. I. Title.
  BL435.J64 2002
  291.4—dc21

                            2002010518

10 9 8 7 6 5 4 3 2
Manufactured in the United States of America

SkyLight Paths Publishing is creating a place where people of different spiritual traditions come together for challenge and inspiration, a place where we can help each other understand the mystery that lies at the heart of our existence.

SkyLight Paths sees both believers and seekers as a community that increasingly transcends traditional boundaries of religion and denomination—people wanting to learn from each other, *walking together, finding the way.*

SkyLight Paths, "Walking Together, Finding the Way" and colophon are trademarks of LongHill Partners, Inc. registered in the U.S. Patent and Trademark Office.

Walking Together, Finding the Way
Published by SkyLight Paths Publishing
An Imprint of Turner Publishing Company
4507 Charlotte Avenue, Suite 100
Nashville, TN 37209
Tel: (802) 457-4000
www.skylightpaths.com

may the wind deal kindly w/ us
may the fire remember our names
may springs flow, rain fall again
may the land grow green, may it swallow our mistakes

—From "Life Chant" by Diane Di Prima

Contents

Air   143

Preface

> I am the taste of pure water and the radiance of the sun and moon.
> I am the sacred word and the sound heard in air, and the courage
> of human beings. I am the sweet fragrance in the earth and the
> radiance of fire; I am the life in every creature and the striving
> of the spiritual aspirant.
> —THE BHAGAVAD GITA

While we have so very much in common as humans, our religious differences, especially, often serve to alienate us from one another. Every day we are bombarded by reminders of the violent harm that people do to each other, frequently in the name of faith. But there is a place where we are more connected than estranged, more linked than sundered. If we go deep, to the place that is older than the branches, twigs, and leaves of the global religions, we find the root where all our widely differing paths are one.

The root of human spirituality is grounded in four elements—earth, water, fire, and air. They are common to all people and to virtually every spiritual path; they are how we have understood and celebrated the Great Mystery since there were humans to do so. This prehistoric concept of four elements eventually surfaced in the mythologies of every ancient civilization, from the Sumerians to the Hindus, from the Native North and South Americans to the ancient Egyptians, Greeks, and Romans. The ancient Chinese included metal and wood in addition to earth, water, and fire, but air is there as well, since everything is thought to spring from *ch'i*, related to air, the breath, and the life force in all things. A few other traditions also include mention of a fifth element: ether, or aether, which is the *prima materia*, a spiritual essence of which the immortal bodies of angels or gods are made, or the divine spirit imbuing all things, much like the Chinese *ch'i*.

The elements relate in every culture to the four directions and to the four generally accepted ways of disposing of the dead; eventually, they gave birth to the idea of four bodily "humors" that classify human behavior, four suits of Tarot cards (and, later, playing cards), and even, perhaps, Carl Jung's four basic personality types. They are the building blocks of human understanding.

When we explore and savor and interact with these elements, we are both remembering a primal connection and forging it anew. Welcome, then, to this travel guide for a journey with a particular purpose: connecting with the elements that are so basic and universal to all of us. We will look at the many ways that different faiths have danced with earth, water, fire, and air throughout history, coming to a deeper appreciation of each way's uniqueness and a greater respect for one another's paths, at the same time remembering the commonality of our human beginnings.

While the information in this book is by no means scholarly or exhaustive, I trusted that if I was surprised or fascinated by something I found in my own journey through the world's religions, you would be, too. And all of my work—including my other books and the healing work I do with my counseling clients—is grounded in love for earth, water, fire, and air. I have seen at first hand how deeply nourishing it can be to live in an elemental way. It is this rich, elemental juiciness I want to share with you.

For those of us actively seeking a more satisfying and personal connection to spirit, this book offers guided visualizations, meditations, journal questions, and creative ideas that will help you find your own way in to each element. Some of the activities are perfect for groups to try together. My own life is enriched by an association with several groups; they were the seedbed of many of the ideas in this book. Here is a favorite circle song from one of them:

Earth my body
Water my blood
Air my breath and
Fire my spirit.

When I taught a week-long earth-honoring workshop recently to a large group of children who ranged in age from four to twelve, it was this song that gathered us all together. The elements were our framework: every day we explored earth, water, fire, or air—making ceremonies, singing, creating magical art from simple things we found in nature. During that week I really saw the power of the elements to create a loving community from individuals of very different ages, backgrounds, and faiths.

And so, although I set out to write a book about the elements, I found instead that in some mysterious way, the elements were writing me. The entire project has been attended by wonderful synchronicities too numerous to mention; suffice it to say that the hand of Mystery has been very present all along, dropping just what was needed into my lap, opening books to just the right pages, leading me to meet helpful people and have perfect elemental encounters, over and over again. I have emerged from the experience with an even deeper understanding of how earth, water, fire, and air inform my life, how they shape me, use me, and want to be expressed through me. It is a journey for which I am profoundly grateful. I offer it to you now. May it give us a deeper connection to one another, to our own spirits, to this beautiful and sacred planet.

> We shall not cease from exploration
> And the end of all our exploring
> Will be to arrive where we started
> And know the place for the first time.
> —T. S. ELIOT

Acknowledgments

I gratefully acknowledge the following for permission to include the longer excerpts of poetry in this book:

Coleman Barks, for permission to reprint excerpts from his masterful translations of Rumi.

Wesleyan University Press for permission to reprint the excerpt from Antonio Machado's "Last Night," translated by Robert Bly and published in *Times Alone: Selected Poems of Antonio Machado*, copyright ©1983.

The Regents of the University of California for permission to reprint the excerpt from Charles Olson's "These Days," from *The Collected Poems of Charles Olson*, edited by George Butterick and published by the University of California Press, copyright ©1987.

New Directions Publishing Corporation for permission to reprint the excerpt from Kenneth Rexroth's "Hojoki" from *Collected Shorter Poems*, copyright ©1966 by Kenneth Rexroth.

Irene Young, for permission to reprint her poem, "A Mermaid Knows," copyright ©1996 by Irene Young.

Many thanks to Maura D. Shaw for her brilliant ideas, her insightful and expert editing, and her treasured friendship which is one of the nourishing joys of my life. Loving thanks also to Joe Bartusis for sharing both his extensive library and his knowledge of Buddhism and yoga, and also for his thoughtful support and great cooking. In some mysterious way, his presence facilitated this book. Thanks to my son, Reid Hannan, for following his own path and occasionally keeping me company on mine, and to my parents, Pat and Bob Johnson, whose unfailing enthusiasm for any project of mine is greatly appreciated. My deep gratitude to Susan Millen, the good fairy of my spirit, and to Elizabeth Cunningham: valuable resource, perceptive reader, and soul-friend.

My loving and heartfelt thanks to the following people who lent books, sent informational e-mails, offered healing, information, inspiration, and support of many kinds: Darshano Alba, Ania Aldrich, Gigi Alvaré, Peter Blum, David Budd, Lara Chkhetiani, Ruth Cook, Santha Cooke, Tom Cowan, Karen Holtslag, Ashling Kelly, Farah Shaw Kelsey, Jack Maguire, Kathleen Mandeville, Dennis McCarthy, Rhianna Mirabello, Lila Pague, Maggie Pickard, Johanne Renbeck, Nancy Rowe, Swami Saradananda, Gary Seigel, Sandy Sklar, Douglas Smyth, Marina Smyth, Regina-Sophia, Joe Tantillo, and Cynthia Trapanese—and to the High Valley community for dancing, singing, and sharing.

Finally, for the excellence, warmth, and heart of their entire team, to Jon Sweeney, Stuart M. Matlins, Emily Wichland, Lauren Seidman, Anna Chapman, and the designers at SkyLight Paths, many, many thanks.

Earth

Introducing Earth

whatever you have to say, leave
the roots on, let them
dangle

And the dirt

    Just to make clear
    where they come from.
—CHARLES OLSON[1]

W e begin our journey through the elements with the one that is our ground. Although it seems that we are formed as if by magic inside our mothers' bodies, we arrive on this planet already intimate with the element that is synonymous with it, the deep matter of our existence. We are flesh of its flesh, bone of its bone, made of its minerals, its very substance. We feed upon it; it gives us everything we need.

Earth is one of the two "safe" elements: unlike water and fire, potentially fatal even in small doses, except for rare instances of mudslide or earthquake, earth is steady, solid, and reliable. But even though it may be safe, earth isn't necessarily easy. Its terrain is so varied that we often lose sight of the fact that it is all one thing. Do you remember the first time we saw those photographs of the earth taken from the moon? Suddenly we *got* it: this is a small planet, round and perfect and precious. Territories disappeared, boundaries between countries disappeared, and what remained was a vision of wholeness. But seen close up, earth is an undulating panorama: plants rise and fall, endlessly flowering and fruiting in wave after wave of life; broad plains and gentle hills soar up to spires of stone, their summits ringed with clouds. Deserts shimmering in a haze of heat, lush and fruitful valleys, forests with their canopies woven of infinite diversity, polar realms of ice—earth encompasses it all. Always changing, always the same, it is seedbed, cornucopia, *home*.

Earth covers a lot of ground, as it were, encompassing the ever-lasting solidity of stone, rock, and mountain, and also the soil, dirt, the humble humus and all things rooted in it—trees, plants, our food. The earth element also includes the creatures who live upon it, since, when they die, their bodies go back to it and become it once again: an end-less circle of life feeding on life, life rising up from death. We *are* the earth, and we walk upon the dust of unknown generations.

Many of us have been raised in religious traditions that honor mind and spirit over this very physical, undeniably dirty element, but its quiet strength underlies even Judeo-Christian customs. In the handful of dirt thrown on the coffin, the stone placed on the head-stone after each visit, the smudge of ash on the forehead once a year, even the very altars of our churches and synagogues, earth quietly asserts itself as the ground beneath it all.

Earth invites us to discover the essential ways that people have understood this rich element throughout time, by going on a delicious adventure. It begins with the fertile mother-ground that gives us nour-ishment, but the trip will include some deep digging, too, for earth is also the underground. As Pulitzer Prize–winning author Annie Dillard says, "Ours is a planet sown in beings. Our generations overlap like shingles. We don't fall in rows like hay, but we fall. Once we get here, we spend forever on the globe, most of it tucked under." For people throughout the ages, under-earth has been the Dark Place, home of the dead, sometimes seen as a place of terrible punishment—or as a mysterious realm of discovery.

Earth is also the monumental solidity of rock, outlasting us by ages. From time immemorial, humans have raised and worshipped holy stones; together, we will find and circumambulate a few. We will also peer into the shadowy caves of our ancestors and remember being held safely in earth's embrace. We will make a pilgrimage to the very spirit of Mountain, dedicated both to aspiring and to staying still. Finally, we will gather in sacred groves and lush garden paradises, to dance in praise of earth's numinous beauty.

Unearthing the ways this element has been known and celebrated throughout time will help us find our own grounding, our own unique place in earth's eternal round dance, the endless circle of being.

Earth Prayer

Root of the root,
Mother Matter, for whom nothing is ever lost,
only transformed,
you teach us how to change
and how to sit in stillness.
When life scatters us in all directions
you whisper, "Just be."
You urge us, "Honor the body."
You tell us, "I will never let you go, I hold you safe forever."
All praise to the humble holy ground.
We are part of you no less
than seed or grass or antelope.
We belong.
May we learn new ways to honor you.
May our presence here be of benefit to you.
May we heal the harm we have done to you.
In the name of earth,
Be so.

1

The Nurturing Ground

Our first real experience of earth is our mother's body, the smell and texture of her skin, the landscapes of her hills and valleys, the nourishment she gives that is synonymous with love and caring. Like water, earth is often considered female, maternal; throughout the world, our earliest stories about earth are stories of a generous, loving Mother.

> The earth is at the same time mother,
> ....
> She is the mother of all,
> for contained in her
> are the seeds of all.
> —HILDEGARD OF BINGEN (TRANSLATED BY GABRIELE UHLEIN)

In his "Hymn to the Earth," Homer, too, describes the earth as the mother of all, "splendid as rock," nourishing everything. But in slightly later stories, the bodies of mother goddesses are torn apart and scattered, becoming food. Open *The Golden Bough*, that seminal work on human culture, to nearly any page that discusses some of the still later practices around earth and food, and we uncover a nightmare of violence: human sacrifice, bloodletting, flaying, and dismemberment were how many people sought to ensure the land's fertility. We need to remember that it wasn't always so.

Once we roamed the earth in small groups, picking and gathering and then moving on. The ability to stay rooted in one spot of earth came from witnessing a miracle: when the dead seed is planted, it lives again. Suddenly, like deities, we could make things grow. We could plant and harvest and stay in one place. Many of the earliest agricultural people honored a sacred and benevolent Mother Goddess who provided for her children abundantly; in lush Paleolithic Western Europe, many small goddess statues were carved in her honor.[1] But as time wore on, humans multiplied, cooperation was replaced by violent competition for land and resources, the ways of the Mother were lost, and the stories were twisted. Once all-powerful goddesses were raped, killed, married off to "superior" father-gods, or suppressed and hidden away altogether beneath the surface of our consciousness.

Some agricultural people adopted the idea of a king who was the lover of the land, a sacrificial king whose blood watered the earth so that the crops could grow; death-and-resurrection gods echoed the yearly cycle of planting, growth, and harvest. Other groups killed off the glowing spirit of the land altogether, making it a chattel, a soulless thing for humans to dominate and use.

Beliefs shape our reality. Today, people create a toxic and polluted environment as the direct result of a belief that earth is our possession, inferior (some would even say evil) and dead, only worth its resources, only as good as the immediate profit to be gained from it. But once, long ago, *all* people believed that earth is sacred. As humans we share that common heritage. If we could re-embrace the idea of earth as living, ensouled, and holy, then our attitudes toward it would surely shift in healing ways.

To help us re-envision healthier beliefs about the earth, let's walk for a moment on some spiritual paths that teach respectful and loving relationship to it. In Shinto, the indigenous religion of Japan, the preindustrial people lived in such harmony with the natural world that they had no separate word for nature. Today, Shinto still teaches that the sacred is both immanent and transcendent: the divine is everywhere. The principles of Shinto are reflected in the growing number of Japanese citizens' groups to combat pollution and industrial disease and to preserve the environment.

Countless shrines to *kami*—spirits that evoke awe—exist throughout Japan. Many shrines unobtrusively pay homage to sites of natural power and beauty; we find them tucked away beside sacred trees, rock crevices, or waterfalls.

There is a palpable sense of harmony and peace as well as great beauty in the Shinto aesthetic. A Shinto-style garden was one of my favorite haunts when my son, then a toddler, and I lived in Brooklyn. There, a path led over a stream to a lake, where we would pause on an arched footbridge—its wooden rails smooth and warm under our hands—to watch gleaming carp lazily weaving in and out of sight. So many shades of restful green ringed that lake; willows, Japanese maples, other trees with shiny heart-shaped leaves rustled quietly in the wind. Large rocks were placed carefully here and there—rocks with a very imposing and solid presence. Every time our eyes came to rest on them, we felt a comforting sense of grounded strength. Eventually, the path wound its way up a steep hill thick with evergreens. The fallen needles quieted our footsteps, and the sweet pine scent was so soothing that I could feel the tensions and noise of the city gently falling away from me with every step. But our favorite part of the garden was the *kami* shrine at the summit of the hill. Young as he was, Reid could sense the magic in that small wooden structure; we could feel how it honored the essence of that place.

The worship of *kami* is meant to bring human life into *kannagara*, or harmony with nature. (Interestingly, *kannagara* is also the word for the movements of the heavenly bodies.) Jangled and stressed from city life as I so often was, whenever we spent time in the presence of that shrine, and in that place, I could begin to remember my connection to nature again. The deep nourishment that garden gave me helped me to survive my years in the city.

Many indigenous people have never lost their connection with the earth. Sadly, there has been a long-standing tradition among supposedly more "civilized" people to regard tribal groups as backward and "primitive," inferior just like the earth to which they are closely tied. But things are changing in this regard. Now there is intense interest in indigenous ways, or "Original Instructions," in the hope that they may hold the key to living in right relationship with earth.

> Many people have said that indigenous peoples are myths of the past, ruins that have died. But the indigenous community is not a vestige of the past, nor is it a myth. It is full of vitality and has a course and a future. It has much wisdom and richness to contribute. They have not killed us, and they will not kill us now. We are stepping forth to say, "No, we are here. We live."
>
> —RIGOBERTA MENCHU, GUATEMALAN QUICHÉ INDIAN

Imagine for a moment walking beside an Australian Aboriginal or a Lakota Sioux, or a Kenyan Kikuyu. These are very different people, as different as their unique landscapes. But the core beliefs of most indigenous groups are remarkably similar.

Everything is alive and everything is related. Rocks, snakes, streams, and trees are our kindred, part of Spirit, and possessors of information and wisdom that may be communicated to humans. Imagine your heart running and leaping with Deer, knowing that she is your sister. Imagine learning from the shapes and patterns of the stones.

**The earth and everything growing in or on it is
sacred.** Thoughtless destruction or killing is unthinkable. If
a life must be taken—for food, for example—then the act is
performed in a spirit of mindfulness and gratitude, and
nothing is wasted. Imagine your heart opening in thankful-
ness to your garden, to the miracle of each ripe tomato,
each crisp green lettuce leaf. Imagine the numinous holiness
of the ground you walk upon.

Group rituals are vitally important. Together, we bond
with one another, honoring and celebrating the great
Oneness of All. There is a pervading sense of kinship and
interconnectedness rather than disconnection and alien-
ation. Imagine joining hands with others in a circle and
knowing that all are deeply related, that you belong.

Spirit may be experienced directly and often joyfully.
Ecstatic communion with the numinous can happen.
Imagine opening so wide that Spirit sings in you.

Today, many nonindigenous groups embrace a sense of earth as
both sacred and interconnected. Not only deep ecology and ecospiri-
tuality but also Neo-Paganism, sometimes referred to as Wicca or
Witchcraft, hold beliefs closely related to the indigenous "Original
Instructions." Starhawk, in *The Spiral Dance*, explains:

> Witchcraft is a religion, perhaps the oldest religion extant
> in the West. . . . The Old Religion, as we call it, is closer in
> spirit to Native American traditions or to the shamanism of
> the Arctic. . . . Witchcraft takes its teachings from nature,
> and reads inspiration in the movements of the sun, moon,
> and stars, the flight of birds, the slow growth of trees, and
> the cycle of the seasons.

While we seem to be experiencing a rise in divisive and often anti-earth fundamentalism, there is a corresponding growth in the popularity of these earth-centered paths. Perhaps an earth-honoring view is gradually becoming more widely accepted. And it is important to remember how passionately it is possible for humans to love a homeland. Wars always have been—and still are—fought over bits of earth, not only for their resources but because they are so vitally important to their inhabitants. Warring people often demonize and disconnect from one another. But, as Joseph Campbell said, "Today, the planet is the only proper 'in group.'"

> May we remember that we are all made of you,
> great earth.
> Because you wanted hands, you called us forth.
> Because walking was needed, you called us forth.
> Because you wanted life to be renewed again and again,
> you made us long for one another.
> We are your hands, your legs, your radiant flesh.
> All of us are made of you.
> May we remember.

Joyous relationship with earth is our birthright. When my son was an infant, I took him to a park and placed him on the ground for the very first time. He clutched the grass in both hands and beamed, look-ing, said a friend, "as if he had come home." Later, I carried him back to our city apartment to change him and laughed when I found that a blade of grass had worked its way into his diaper. It seemed like a sign that he had been claimed by the primal Great Mother, perfectly woven into her web, one with all that is. These activities and meditations are designed to give us our own direct experience of earth's nourishing richness.

Being with the Earth

Sometimes the best part of the journey is simply sitting still. In stillness, we can open, put down spirit-roots, find our own way in to the dark seedbed. We can feel our ancient connection to this motherland, to the element that is our ground.

Once, people went to sacred places in nature, sometimes living alone for days in order to gather wisdom and feel their oneness with the All. If you have the luxury of taking time to go camping, do. But even if time is short, you can pick a pleasant day and spend an hour simply sitting still on the earth, near a tree if possible. Slow down. Breathe. Notice everything. What tiny plants are growing near you? Do you see any insects? What does the breeze feel like in your hair? What rhythms are you aware of, in the wind or the swaying of the trees? Sense the earth underneath you.

Mother, I can feel you under my feet.
Mother, I can hear your heartbeat.[2]

You may want to lie down and experience your spine in alignment with the earth. This is a good thing to remember whenever you need grounding: simple physical contact with the earth will help every time. Allow your mind to relax and flow out toward the ground. Imagine the amazing processes going on underneath it at this very moment. Think of all the generations of life that have gone to make up this soil. Picture all the seeds and roots and insects and microbes busy in it. Imagine the roots of the trees reaching down, drawing up nourishment from the dark, their leaves and branches with the veins and capillaries shaped so much like your own. Know that you are made of the same materials as the tree, as the earth. Imagine the spirit of these materials singing quietly all around you.

Where we stand is holy, holy is the ground,
Forest, mountain, river, listen to the sound,
Great Spirit circling all around us.[3]

Feel your essential oneness with tree and ground. Now truly open your eyes and ears, and see what you notice; you may see or hear something of spirit-value to you. Nature often reveals secrets and wisdom to us if we pay attention. Indigenous people have practiced gathering omens in nature for millennia. What does this place have to tell you? Imagine that this bit of earth, these trees know you are here, know who you are, and care for you. Allow yourself to be held gently by the earth.

Growing Earth-Love

Many of us garden or keep houseplants, so we already participate in the act of growing things, but here we are invited to witness the green process with a new kind of heart-centered awareness. Earth is so unbelievably generous. Plant something, take care of it, and it grows. If it's a flower, we can enjoy its beauty. If it's a food plant, we can eat it. We've been stomping on the earth for a while now, spewing our poisons into it, strip-mining it, hacking it to bits. Still, if we find a bit of earth that isn't too ruined, and we plant something in it, it grows. The nourishing Mother simply keeps on creating. And the transition from seed to plant is mind-boggling, when we really stop to think about it. So, grow something. If you don't have access to any arable land, get yourself a flowerpot and some soil.

Now, choose some seeds. Harvest them from a plant, if you can, or buy a packet with a pretty picture on it from the store. Now really look at the seeds. They don't look like much, do they? They're so small and hard and dry. Who would ever guess that green lush gorgeous things live in there? Who could imagine any correspondence between the little pellets lying in the palm of your hand and the delicious picture on the front of the packet? What a stupendous idea seeds are!

Plant the seeds in the soil, say a prayer over them, wish them well, water them, keep them warm and moist. Whenever you pass by, think of them with love. Wonder if the seeds have cracked open in the dark yet. What's going on down there? It's a secret. Are there tiny roots forming? Have the first shoots broken free? It takes a kind of courage to break out of the seed. Does it hurt? Imagine being the seed. Imagine its progress in the dark. When the first green finally appears, applaud. Sing to the new plants, open your heart to them, love them. Care for them. They have so much to teach us. Transformation takes time. Small things can contain great ones. Remember the strength of these seemingly fragile things: weeds can split a concrete sidewalk, ivy can tear down a building. The life force is unbelievably strong. It is in each of us. What will you choose to grow? What image has the most power or juice for you—the seed breaking open, the thrusting of root and shoot, or the first emergence of green? What does this say about who and where you are right now?

The following seed-thoughts are meant to be sat with and mulled over for a while. You may want to take them into the dark bed of your dreams with you. See what comes of them. One may take root and grow into something of unexpected value.

Seed-Thoughts on Earth as Great Nourisher

1. What pleasant childhood memories do you have of earth? The delicious squishy feeling of making mudpies? The smell of the soil after a warm spring rain? Picnics in the grass? Sitting on a sun-baked rock? Digging a hole and sitting in it? Your first garden? Many of us treasure memories of feeling at one with nature when we were small—memories that give us deep soul-nourishment. Remember.

2. Have you ever picked and eaten wild food? There is nothing more satisfying; the sheer pleasure of it is encoded in our genes. Imagine

walking, like our ancient ancestors, through a landscape that we know and love and feel at one with, searching for food. The plants speak, saying, "Look over here. Here we are. We want to be eaten. You will help us spread our seeds." You may want to read a few books on wild-plant foraging. Euell Gibbons's *Stalking the Wild Asparagus* was my handbook in college; the cafeteria food was so bad that I learned to supplement my diet with what I could find, and there was something truly magical in allowing the land to feed me. You may want to try it, too.

3. Our early relationship with our mothers and the food she gave us can help to shape (or distort) our attitudes about our bodies, ourselves, and the earth. What is your infant story? Many of us have chosen to nurse our babies on demand and for as long as they need, but the infants in my generation were mostly bottle-fed; it was considered superior, more scientific. Were you given the gift of that intimate, nourishing contact with your mother? Mine tried to breastfeed me, but she was just too ill and tense. When I really sit with this knowledge, it makes sense that I never quite believe that the seeds I plant will grow, that the garden will produce enough to feed me. When the tomatoes are so lush and heavy that they sag clear down to the ground, I am simply astounded. What are your stories around mother, food, and earth?

4. Find your own sacred landscape. To discover an inner place—a soul-landscape where you feel deeply and completely at home—is one of the most valuable gifts you can give yourself. Once you have found it, you can go there in your mind whenever you are tired or stressed or unhappy and find soul-nourishment. I discovered my spirit-place many years ago, when I was living and working in New York City. I visited it often, and it never failed to give me ease, a sense of peaceful sanctuary. Later, pregnant with my son and riding crowded subways in the steamy city summer, it calmed

and strengthened me. You will be amazed at what a difference this can make for you.

First, become an explorer. This special place has been waiting for you to discover it. Find some time when you will not be disturbed, and sit comfortably with your eyes closed. Play some soft, relaxing music, if you like. Now allow your mind to wander. What landscapes come to mind? Think of all the different kinds you know. Which one makes you feel at home? Does your inner self long for verdant green woods? Plains shimmering with heat? High mountains, where the air is cool and clear and you can see for miles? An ocean shore, where the water is a vivid blue? Or something completely different? Decide where you would like to be, right now, if you could wave a magic wand. A fjord, field, jungle, orchard, tundra—just imagine it. Now walk through this landscape. What are the colors like? What does the air feel like? Smell like? Feel the ground under your feet. What plants do you notice? Find a place to sit, and relax there. If animals appear, notice what they are; they may have deep significance for you. Spend some time simply being in your place. If you wish to invite others there, you certainly can, but always remember that this is *your* landscape. Enjoy it. Visit it as often as you like; soon you will learn your way around. It will be familiar and safe, a refuge that is always there for you whenever you need it.

5. Ponder this excerpt by the great Sufi poet Rumi, here translated by Coleman Barks:

> how will you know the difficulties of being human
> if you're always flying off to blue perfection?
> Where
> will you plant your
> grief-seeds?

We need
ground
to scrape and hoe, not the sky of unspecified desire.
—RUMI[4]

What are the grief seeds—or joy seeds—you wish to plant? You may want to write a few words about your planting process, or find images from magazines or catalogs that evoke what you want to grow. Cut them out and make a collage. When we give something over to Ground, we allow the Great Nurturer to work her transformative magic in our lives.

2

The Underworld

Nearly every group of people throughout history has believed in an underworld. In its simplest form, it is the land of the dead, a neutral region you go to when you die, where the body dissolves and returns to the dirt, and the soul waits for rebirth or just simply exists. Some groups see the underground as a place of punishment for transgression, a terrible realm of suffering and torment, the fear of which ensures that people behave decently. But others have understood it as a place of strange power, *el mundo subterraneo* that Clarissa Pinkola Estés describes in *Women Who Run with the Wolves,* an underground world that is our psychic home, into which we can venture and from which we emerge stronger and wiser.

It takes courage to go down into the dark, but there is much of value to be experienced there. When we hold hands together and begin the descent, we are in good company: shamans and wise ones have made this journey intentionally since before the beginning of time. A deep way of knowing lives in the shadow places. When we learn our way around in the dark, we make peace with death. And we return to the world above ground renewed, strengthened, and less afraid.

To agricultural people throughout the world, so closely tied to the cycles of planting, reaping, and planting again, burial in the earth echoed a hope of being reborn like the spring. We have learned much of what we know about early people by the burial sites they leave behind. Many corpses lie curled in fetal position, covered with red pigment like birth-blood, and surrounded by tools, food—everything needed for a new life. Burial was a return to the womb of the Mother. The early underworld realm was female.

Patricia Monaghan lists no fewer than sixty-six underworld goddesses in her *Book of Goddesses and Heroines*. One exemplar is the Norse Hel, who is, according to Clarissa Pinkola Estés, a goddess not only of death but of life; she teaches the dead to live backward, becoming younger and younger until they are ready to be reborn. Hel's realm had several "circles," like the Catholic place of punishment to which she gave her name, as Dante described it. But that is where the similarity ends. As Joseph Campbell pointed out, for pre-Christian people "the intelligence in the center of the earth was not satanic but divine." Hel's name is "not only cognate with the term hell, but also with holy, heal, hallow, hello, whole, all, halo, and holly."[1] Ironically, she appears to be related to Holla, originally a hearth-fire goddess, who may have been one source for the idea of burning hellfires.

The concept of a punitive underground hell is certainly not, however, exclusively Christian but is found in virtually every major global religion: Buddhists, Hindus, Jews, and Muslims all have some idea of it. Interestingly, although other indigenous people, such as the African Gabon, or Fon, share in this concept, Native Americans, for the most part, do not.

Classical Buddhism identified seven "hot hells" surrounded by torture chambers, including a fiery pit. Tibetan Buddhists added eight "cold hells" to these, as well as the idea of peripheral hells for those whose sins were less severe. The Hindu Mankadeya Purana also speaks of seven hells; the Rig Veda describes a "lowest darkness" and a deep pit into which are cast false men and faithless women.

Another notion of seven distinct hells appears in the Muslim Qur'an, and most of them are fiery, so we will revisit them when we come to the element of fire. Their names include Sair (Blazing Fire), Sagar (Scorching Fire), and al-Jahim (Fierce Fire). The Hebrew Scripture speaks only of a final trial of the earth by fire: "For a fire is kindled by my anger, and it burns to the depths of Sheol, devours the earth and its increase, and sets on fire the foundations of the mountains" (Deuteronomy 32:22). The original Sheol was not a torture-chamber but simply the under-earth abode of the dead, a place of silence. Eventually, however, Sheol became identified with the Muslim Gehenna, a realm of punishment introduced to the Jews, scholars think, by Iranian doctrines. Until the third century C.E., rabbinical teachings reserved eternal torment for only the most heinous of sinners, but later teachings identified several sections of hell, where appropriate punishments would be meted out to different types of sinners. This later concept carried over into the apocalyptic visions we associate with Peter and Paul, hence into Christian ideology.

Some traditions claim that Christ descended to the underworld after his crucifixion, where he "harrowed hell" and then came back above ground. As long as people believe in an underground realm of punishment or death, there will always be stories of those who manage to thwart fate, going to the place of no return—and returning.

One of the most ancient of these stories is that of the Sumerian goddess Inanna. Here is a retelling of it:

> It all begins when Inanna decides to go visit her sister Erishkegal, the Queen of the Underworld. Erishkegal has been recently widowed and is in deep mourning. The rather self-involved and unthinking Inanna seems more motivated by wanting to beat the odds by going to the Dark Place and coming back than by any concern for her sister. Anyway, down she goes. She passes seven gates (there's that mystical

number seven again, the number of hells in so many traditions), and at each gate she is forced to give something up: her necklace, her ring, her armband, her crown. Finally, stripped naked, she arrives before her sister, who, unamused by Inanna's bravado, gives her the Dead Eye and hangs her on a meathook. And there Inanna stays. Fortunately for her, she has left instructions with a friend above ground on what to do in case she doesn't come back. Three days and three nights go by, and there's no sign of Inanna, so the friend goes into action: off she runs to three father-gods and begs them for help. Two of them just roll their eyes and say, "We told her not to go; it's her own fault; forget about it." But the kindly Enki makes two little beings from the dirt under his fingernails to send down after Inanna. These little crud-beings sit with the grieving Erishkegal and really listen to her, mourn with her, weep with her; they are, perhaps, the first therapists. Relieved at having finally been heard, she agrees to let Inanna go. The dirt-beings give Inanna some reviving food and drink, and up they all go to the world above ground, where Inanna must find a substitute to send down in her place. She refuses to send her loyal friend or her children. Who can she possibly choose? Then she sees her lover, Dumuzi, who has had the audacity to sit on her throne in her absence, dandling dancing girls upon his knee, no doubt. She gives him the Dead Eye, and down he goes. But Dumuzi's loving sister insists on taking his place for six months out of every year, in a deal very much reminiscent of the bargain made by Persephone (an ancient Greek goddess who lives for six months of each year with her husband in the underworld, because she ate six pomegranate seeds on her first visit there), so the story has a relatively happy ending.

In *When the Drummers Were Women*, Layne Redmond quotes songs and poetic fragments that show both Inanna and Persephone finding their way back from the underworld by following the sound of drumming. This leads us very neatly to the realm of shamans, for whom drumming is also a vehicle of choice, enabling them to travel between worlds. Shamans sometimes journey to an Upper World, often by means of smoke or by climbing the World Tree, but it is the underworld journey with which they are most closely associated.

Under the earth I go
On an oak leaf I stand
I ride the filly that was never foaled
I carry the dead in my hand.
—CELTIC SHAMAN-SONG[2]

Most people do their utmost to avoid the underworld. Staying alive, staying topside, is what matters, what one stretches every nerve and sinew to do. Shamans do not run away from the nightmare monster; they go after it. They *choose* to go under. And they learn things there that heal others, that inspire whole clans or tribes. They are the seers, the visionaries, accessing knowledge in nonordinary ways from nonordinary realities, and bringing it back for the good of all. As Joan Halifax says in *Shaman: The Wounded Healer*, "The shaman is self-slain through the surrender of all that is transient, becoming like a great field that is plowed, ripped open for seed to be planted."

The earliest known human works of art are Paleolithic cave-paintings of shamans; the concept of braving the dark in order to learn its secrets is as old as humanity. The branches of our global religions may differ widely, but when we dig around in the dirt beside the treetrunks, we uncover the intertwining shamanic roots.

I invite you to try the following guided meditation, patterned after the traditional underground journey of the shaman. We live in a rootless, arid culture, which feeds not our deepest spirit-hungers but only a frenzy to buy more, consume more, spend more money. When we begin consciously rooting around, examining the structure of our support system, we can begin to draw up the nourishment we need from the deep and magical power of our mother-planet, from the rich realm of underground.

Yes I'm here to heal
With the healing ways
Of the Magic-of-the-Ground
And the Magic-of-the-Earth
—YUKAGHIR SHAMAN-SONG[3]

Underground Journey to the Roots

This guided meditation offers vital information on our own deep support system and its ability to gather the soul-food we crave from the fertile power of our earth connection. We start the healing process at the root level.

Before you begin, you will need to choose an entryway. It may be an actual place in nature that you have seen, or one that exists only in your imagination, but it is generally a threshold, opening, or betwixt-and-between place. Some examples might be the hollow of an old tree, the place where wick touches flame or stone meets soil, the back of a waterfall, or an ancient well. Have the image of this place in your mind before you go. You may want to make an audiotape of this meditation, or have a friend read it to you, so you can really relax and enter into it. Remember that journeying, like anything else, gets easier with practice. And you will want to have a journal and pen next to you to write down all the details of your experience after you get back, before they slip away out of memory.

Begin with your heartbeat. Just hold your awareness of it gently, like a flower, in your mind. What is your pulse doing? Can you feel it? Is it quick, or slow, or something in between? Our heartbeat keeps us such good company every step of the way. It is with us now. It can lead us deeper. Begin to imagine your entryway now. See yourself standing in front of it, noticing every detail of it. When you are ready, go through. If you need to grow small to do this, you can.

Now you find yourself in a tunnel underground. It is a warm, dry earth tunnel with a smooth dirt floor. You walk down this tunnel, noticing the earthy smell all around you, the texture of the dirt beneath your feet. The walls may feel rough or smooth to your hands, passing by. You go down and down and down, deeper and deeper and deeper into the earth. The journey is very gentle, the slope downward very gentle, but it takes you down, deeper and deeper into the earth. Now, far ahead of you, you can see a doorway of some kind. It may be an archway of stone, or a carved oaken door, or a curtain of beads, or something else entirely. You approach this doorway. Now you open it and go through.

You are standing in a different place. Look around you and notice anything you can. What season is it here? What is the landscape like? Stand firmly in this place, allowing the sun to shine on your face. As you stand here, imagine that there are roots growing from the bottoms of your feet, roots reaching down into the soil, roots that keep your spirit firmly anchored, roots that keep you from being knocked over by strong winds, roots that draw up nourishment and energy from the earth. Imagine going down through the soil along with these roots, down and down and branching out on all sides. How are your roots? What are they like? Are they thin and threadlike or thick and vital? What color are they? How far do they spread, underground? Do they reach deep? Notice how your root system looks and feels. Does it seem strong and secure? Imagine your roots growing thicker, more lush, spreading out underground, forming a beautiful network of support for you. Imagine how they pull delicious earthy nourishment up from the depths of the underground for you—energy to make you feel safe, healthy, and juicily alive. Thank your roots for the work they do.

Now, as you look at the rich, dark soil around the roots, you may notice a buried treasure that is meant just for you. Take it with you as you bring your awareness back up from the roots. Now you turn away, knowing that you can come back to visit your roots any time you need to feel more grounded or energized. Walk away from them now, heading back toward the tunnel. Go through the doorway.

Now you are back inside the tunnel, going up, heading up and up quickly through this earthen tunnel, up and up until you are back in this room, back in your body, back to your heartbeat. Stretch your fingers and toes, and open your eyes.

What did you learn about your support system? Remember that you can work consciously to improve and maintain your roots.

> Yet no matter how deeply I go down into myself
> My God is dark, and like a webbing made
> Of a hundred roots that drink in silence.
> —RAINER MARIA RILKE[4]

Seed-Thoughts on Earth as Underworld

1. Many, many of us have undergone descent experiences similar to that of the goddess Inanna's, where we feel gradually stripped of everything familiar or safe, sometimes even losing our own self-concept as we stumble around in the dark. Back before I left my long-term relationship, before it was even clear to my conscious mind that I would have to go, I began working with the Inanna story. I journeyed to her, read the ancient poem that survives about her, found myself drawn to lapis lazuli, her stone. Working with a group, I helped to build a labyrinth, that above-ground

symbol of descent and reemergence. When the time finally came to end the relationship, I discovered that I had done some work in advance. The dark journey wasn't quite as terrifying. I was prepared, knew the way, recognized guideposts: "Oh," I would think, "this is the part where I think I will never get out of this place. This is where I think I've made a wrong turn. This is where I feel completely alone."

What were your times of dark descent? When we are forced to deal with loss, with death, with the necessity of remaking our lives from the roots up, sometimes we have to go deep first. Honor yourself for the underground journeys you have made.

2. Have you ever seen a time-lapse film of something dead undergoing the process of decaying? It is strange and fascinating to watch. The form often swells up initially, but gradually its physical integrity collapses. It dissolves, flattens, and is released back into the soil, food for myriad life-forms. When we really take note of this nitty-gritty course of death/life, we may learn something useful about our own process. For all of us, there is dead "stuff" that needs to be released and transformed so that it can compost our growing.

Pay attention to your own backyard compost heap, if you have one. When you empty your fresh compost onto the pile, take note of what has gone on there since last time. Watch for changes. Nothing is ever wasted in nature. Nothing is ever lost, just recycled. Give some thought to the issues you need to release and transform. You may want to write them down on a piece of dried orange peel and add it to the compost pile. Keep an eye on it. It will change.

3. For many of us, animals gave us our first childhood experience of death. When my son was four, he found a dead bird in the backyard and became visibly upset. After talking a little and simply being with the bird together, we ended up burying it under a favorite tree. We sang a circle song while we did, adding two new lines at the very end:

We all come from the Mother
And to her we shall return,
Like a drop of rain
Flowing to the ocean.
Hoof and horn, hoof and horn,
All that dies shall be reborn.
Claw and wing, claw and wing,
All that flew shall rise and sing.

How did your parents explain death to you? What are your memories around death when you were small? How do you understand death now? What are your beliefs around it?

4. You may want to read about shamanism; it can be an invaluable spiritual practice, as Celtic shaman Tom Cowan has pointed out in his excellent books. Workshops and groups dedicated to learning and practicing shamanic techniques are springing up all over the country. Find one. Our society needs all the help and healing it can get.

5. Who are your ancestors? Where did they live? What were their names? Find out all you can about them; they are part of your root system, part of your very bones. Sometimes we carry their stories in our bodies, unknowing, repeating their patterns until we free ourselves by understanding, releasing, and healing them; but stories of our foremothers can be empowering, too. Several years ago, I suddenly became fascinated by an ancestor of mine, a young woman named Susana White. She was pregnant when she left England with her husband and young son. She gave birth to that second child on a tiny, crowded ship anchored just off the coast of the New World. That first winter in the colonies, every third person she knew died, including her husband. But she survived. I have her tenacity and will to live as part of my very rootstock, and I am deeply grateful to her. What are the strengthening stories in your mother-line?

3

The Sacred Stone

Lift up the stone, you will find Me there.

—GOSPEL OF THOMAS

Our earliest ancestors honored the sacredness of stone, perhaps partly because, unlike everything else in life, it appears to last forever. It has the stamp of eternity about it; it will be around long after we have returned to dust. As a species we do not easily embrace change; we need things that last, and so people everywhere have praised stone's steady, reliable presence.

Throughout time, wherever rock can be found, large ones have been transported, erected, carved, placed in circles, had shrines built to house them, and have been loved, venerated, and worshipped by people. The mystical power of stone crosses all cultural, ethnic, racial, and religious boundaries. For humans everywhere, rocks are both solid and reassuring, and their strength inspires awe.

Most megaliths were in place long before any written record, so the world of intentionally placed stone is often quite mysterious. We don't really know who built the great stone circles or who carved and raised the *moai* on Easter Island. We are also uncertain *how* they did it. Many of the stones are massive; how on earth did ancient people move them? The huge rocks used in the construction of Stonehenge, for example, evidently were brought from over a hundred miles away. And once they somehow managed to get the stones to the right location, how did people with only the most basic technology succeed in raising them into place? And what purpose did they serve? Some dolmens—upright stones with a rooflike slab on top—are memorials to the dead, their magnificent bulk standing guard over burial chambers where bodies slowly returned to the earth, an outgrowth of the age-old practice of piling smaller stones on top of graves to keep wild animals from disturbing them. But the purpose of other stone structures, some quite complex, is unknown. Did they chart the progress of the stars and planets? Were they used in religious rituals? These giant stones often raise more questions than they answer, and yet their sheer presence is an answer that goes beyond any questioning. They simply, magnificently, *are*—and so they have remained for all these many centuries.

There is an ancient rock at the very center of Muslim worship: the Black Stone, a meteorite housed by the Ka'bah, the sacred cube-shaped building that is the focus of pilgrimage to Mecca. The veneration of this stone predates Islam and probably began in the days of Abraham and his son Ishmael, whom Arabs believe to be their ancestor. Legend has it that the stone was given to Adam when he fell from paradise and that it was originally white; it is believed to have become black by absorbing the sins of all the pilgrims who have touched and kissed it. The stone is set into the eastern wall of the Ka'bah and is covered by a brocaded curtain. As the faithful circumambulate the building seven times, they touch, kiss, or salute the stone as they pass. Imagine being part of the huge crowd circling the stone, your fingers brushing it, feeling its cool smoothness, knowing how many thousands upon thousands of people have touched it, for how many hundreds upon hundreds of years. Stone connects us to our ancestors. It was around when they were; somehow it contains their presence. And meteorites are doubly wonderful, since they fall from the sky like a gift from some higher, greater power.

Hindus, too, revere special stones. They are called lingams and are associated with the god Shiva, and while they are smooth and upright, they are not merely phallic symbols but are representative of Shiva's transcendently creative nature. Like the Black Stone in the Ka'bah, Shiva-lingams are the object of pilgrimages by tens of thousands of people every year. Devotees anoint the stones with sandalwood paste, honey, or clarified butter, and they offer them gifts of flowers and rose-water. Some lingams are created by human hands, but others are naturally occurring, smoothed by centuries of river water, or formed of ice in remote Himalayan caves. Many are housed by special shrines, often built of stone, where the air is sweet with incense. I recently found a photograph of one such shrine that completely captured my imagination: the lingam itself was lit by direct sunlight, while the simple rock walls that surrounded it remained in shadow. This particular lingam had been an object of worship for more than fourteen centuries; it seemed to exude a solid but very potent energy.

The Hebrew Scripture contains dozens of references to the stability of rock, often equating it with God: "The Lord is my rock and my fortress, and my deliverer, my God my rock, in whom I take refuge" (Psalm 18:2). Christians may not have specific rocks that they venerate, but the very word recalls the name of Peter, that apostle who was the rock upon which Jesus declared he would build his church. Jesus himself, in the old gospel hymn, is said to be the "rock of ages," cleft like a mountainside, a cave for his followers to shelter in.

I am an indestructible fortress,
I am an unassailable rock,
I am a precious jewel.
—OLD IRISH PRAYER[1]

Caves are how people have understood the safety of stone since the beginning of the beginning. Without caves, our ancestors would have perished in the Ice Age. These early people must have accepted the earth's generous and motherly shelter with profound gratitude. Certainly, they carved and painted works of numinous beauty and spirit-power on the cave walls—works that hold a vitally important key for us today. As author and scholar Rachel Pollack has observed:

> Prehistoric cultures understood both the practicality of stones and their spiritual power. If they had not carved and painted their sacred images on rocks and caves we would not know that art, religion, science and sophisticated symbol systems go back tens of thousands of years. From their hard work in creating the rock paintings and stone circles we learn two vital truths—that there is no such thing as a "primitive" human being, and that the soul travels to spirit through the work we do in the reality of the Earth and our own bodies.[2]

Here is Joseph Campbell's own experience of one of these painted caves, which he calls "temple caves":

> Here you come into an enormous chamber, like a great cathedral, with all these painted animals. The darkness is inconceivable. We are there with electric lights, but in a couple of instances the man who was showing us through turned off the light, and you were never in darker darkness in your life. It was—I don't know, just a complete knockout. You don't know where you are, whether you are looking at north, south, east, or west. All orientation is gone, and you are in a darkness that never saw the sun. Then they turn the lights on again, and you see these gloriously painted animals. And they are painted with the vitality of ink on silk in a Japanese painting—you know, just like that. A bull that

will be twenty feet long, and painted so that its haunches will be represented by a swelling in the rock. They take account of the whole thing.[3]

Certainly, caves are associated with an intensity of power; for millennia, many spiritual practices have revolved around them. For instance, they were so centrally important to the rites of Mithra that if no natural cave could be found at a temple site, the followers would dig one. Biblical scrolls have been discovered in caves. Many believe that Christ was buried in a cave, its mouth covered by a huge stone, which was later rolled aside by his resurrection. Hindu *gompas*, or holy hermitages, were first established in caves: caves were thought to represent the yoni of the Great Mother. To spend time in a cave was a return to the all-mothering womb of earth, a death-rebirth experience. Muhammad, founder of Islam, was said to take periodic retreats in a cave on Mount Hira outside Mecca, where he first received the revelations of the Qur'an. In fact, many holy people throughout history are associated with caves. Like Muhammad, Milarepa, the great twelfth-century Tibetan Buddhist poet and saint, favored caves for his meditation retreats. Ferociously dedicated and austere, Milarepa withstood the brutal Himalayan winter eighteen thousand feet up, wearing nothing but a cotton cloth (a *repa*) draped over his body as he sat on bare stone.

> Even on peaks of white snow mountains
> Amidst swirling snow and sleet
> Driven by new year's wintry winds
> This cotton robe burns like fire.[4]

One of Milarepa's meditation caves outside Nyalam has a monastery built around it and is a beloved stop on many pilgrimages, including one made in the late 1990s by Americans Robert Thurman and Tad Wise. They wrote about their Himalayan experiences in *Circling the Sacred Mountain*:

> Out of the hall and off to the side is the spiritual magnet that brought us here in the first place: Milarepa's cave. A most strange room has been built in front of and around it. Concrete buttresses and concrete slabs link the cave with so much of what the hermit radically refused. To the side is the altar covered with photos, money, candles, and incense. The chest-high cave has a shed door at the front, with painted rough idols carved in relief. Mila, green as the nettle stew he ate for years, has one hand cocked to his ear, the other half-covering the withered parsnip of his penis.
>
> The masonry floor gives way to wood, and finally, in back, to the womblike bedrock itself. My flashlight scours the ceiling. Here it is: the pockmark of Mila's holy handprint. My palm fits into it . . .

Today, many hermits, sadhus, and sages inhabit caves throughout the world, living on food offerings left by faithful devotees. Caves are sought out by shamans and earth-honoring people for ceremony and ritual. The secret inner places of earth are still honored as shelter for both body and spirit.

While many caves are subterranean, we are perhaps most familiar with those that are tucked away in the sides of mountains. When we journey up the steep and stony path to visit one of these caves, we are treading on sacred ground already—the sacred ground of mountains, often considered the most holy of places in nearly every religious and spiritual tradition.

What do we know about mountains? They are huge, and ancient beyond ancient. They are forbidding: some are next to impossible to climb, and most are time-consuming to go around. At the top of even a smallish mountain, one can see for miles. The views are breathtaking; they give us perspective. Things definitely feel different on a mountain; the quality of air and wind are not the same as on lower ground. On higher peaks, the thinness of the air makes it both difficult to breathe and easier, perhaps, to have intense spiritual experiences. And mountains are intimately connected to the spirit of many countries: they are the physical feature most easily seen by the most people, even at a great distance.

For both Hindus and Buddhists, the Himalayas—what Tad Wise calls "that gorgeous train wreck of earth"—are sacred. In Hindu mythology, these stupendous mountains are the foothills of Mount Meru, the golden abode of the gods. Although the paths are dangerous—rockslides are common—and the weather unpredictable and harsh, thousands of people make pilgrimages to the mountains every year. Mount Kailash, especially, is a sacred place, thought to be the home of Shiva and his consort Uma.

For many Native Americans, too, mountains are holy, homes of the deities or deities themselves; Gladys A. Reichard lists multiple mountain gods in her *Navaho Religion*. Part of the controversy surrounding the Big Mountain Reservation today is the United States government's desire to mine the area for uranium, although the mountain is considered sacred to the native people. To get some idea of what this means, imagine that someone was to discover there is money to be made in the materials of the Sistine Chapel, or the Ka'bah, or the Western Wall in Jerusalem, so these places must be drilled and stripped, defaced and destroyed.

For religions of transcendence, too, mountains are special; if God is the Most High, then one is closer to God on a mountain. There are rich associations with mountains among Jews, Muslims, and Christians. Moses received the Ten Commandments on Mount Sinai. The Hebrew Scripture is filled with references to mountains, including Psalm 121:1:

I will lift mine eyes unto the hills

From whence cometh my help.

Muhammad received part of the Qur'an on Mount Hira. Jesus delivered one of his greatest sermons on a mountain outside Galilee, and kept a vigil before his arrest and subsequent death in a garden on the Mount of Olives. Several later Christian saints are also said to have lived on mountains, most notably St. Francis of Assisi, who retreated to Mount Alvernia toward the end of his life. Many Christian monasteries are located at the sites of mountain hermitages.

Mountain is also understood as the essence of stillness. I was taught the very simple yoga *asana,* or pose, called "mountain" in a workshop several years ago by one of the teachers at the Institute of Transpersonal Psychology. She used it as an indicator of how grounded (or otherwise) we were. Ideally, the pose should celebrate the perfect poise of stable stillness. At that time in my life (a very painful and difficult one), I learned how much I needed to find my own ground.

Buddhists and Taoists also celebrate Mountain as the emblem of stillness, particularly the stillness of the calm mind. Many Zen masters are associated with the mountains on which they lived, including Ranryo, who explained the relative merits of Zen meditation and Buddha-remembrance as two different mountains, higher and lower potentials dividing a single world:

When they arrive, all alike
See the moon atop the peak,
Only pity those who have no faith
And suffer over the climb.[5]

Buddhist meditation practice is often compared to climbing a mountain, since it can be both physically uncomfortable and tremendously challenging. Climbing mountains is often part of initiatory practices among indigenous people, for the same reasons. Here is Carl

Jung's account of a transformative mountain experience he had as an adolescent, from *Memories, Dreams, Reflections*:

> I was speechless with joy. Here I was at the foot of this mighty mountain, higher than any I had ever seen, and quite close to the fiery peaks of my faraway childhood. I was, indeed, almost a man by now. . . . And now I was to ascend this enormous mountain! I no longer knew which was bigger, I or the mountain. With a tremendous puffing, the wonderful locomotive shook and rattled me up to the dizzy heights where ever-new abysses and panoramas opened out before my gaze, until at last I stood on the peak in the strange thin air, looking into unimaginable distances. . . . It was all very solemn, and I felt one had to be polite and silent up here, for one was in God's world. Here it was physically present.[6]

Thirteenth-century Zen master Dogen, in this translation by Kazuaki Tanahashi, describes some of Mountain's mystique for the spiritual seeker: "Because mountains are high and broad, the way of riding the clouds is always reached in the mountains; the inconceivable power of soaring in the wind comes freely from the mountains."[7]

Both Buddhist and Taoist hermits and poets are associated with their mountain eyries. Consider this excerpt from a poem by Li Pai, which describes climbing Taipai peak in the fading light:

On I went to ride the wind
And reappeared above the clouds
I can nearly touch the moon
No more mountain underneath.[8]

Or, as Sara Klugman says in her poem "God's Body," "the mountains are God's knees."

The following meditations and activities will help you find your own way to celebrate the sacredness of stone in all of its splendid variations.

Rock-Prayer

Several months ago, after the beloved hospice patient he had been visiting almost daily had died, a friend went to a favorite place beside the Hudson River where there are many rocks, some too huge to lift, others easily held in the hand. He was moved to set one large stone on top of a massive one lying half-submerged in the sand. Then he set another on top of that, balancing it all very carefully. The end result was quite beautiful, a sculpture that both drew the eye and rested it. It had the nature of a memorial and also of a prayer. On subsequent trips to the spot, he noticed that someone had added a few smaller stones to the top of his sculpture. Then people began building their own. Eventually, storm and high tide brought them all tumbling down, but those perfectly balanced stones held a special quality of peace and beauty while they lasted. You might want to try making a rock sculpture yourself.

Find a place where there are many stones of different sizes, shapes, textures. Now sit comfortably and just breathe for a little, simply feeling the very different energy of the rocks around you. They are very slow, very still. When you are ready to begin, allow yourself to be guided by what feels right. Which stone wants to be the base, the ground for your prayer sculpture? Now, which one will be steady and safe balanced on top? Continue adding stones—being careful of your fingers and toes—until you feel you have finished. When the rocks don't balance the way we want, or they fall, they teach us valuable lessons in being nonattached to outcome! You may want to say or sing a prayer as you build, or let the building itself be your prayer.

Your children may enjoy this activity, as well. My teenaged son enjoys seeing how many rocks he can balance on top of one another before they come crashing down; one sculpture he made beside a friend's stream is still standing. If you build your sculpture in a public area, you may be pleased and surprised by others' reactions to it. But even if it gets pushed over, your interaction with stone, not the final product, was the devotional activity—and you can repeat it whenever you like.

Cave of Safety

Imagine walking up a stony path on a cliffside. The air is chill, and twilight is approaching. Soon it will be dark, and there are clouds gathering. Rain may be coming, perhaps even snow. You need shelter; you need to feel safe. Imagine that now, ahead and slightly above you on the path, you can see an opening in the cliff face, a narrow doorway, arched and perfect. Soon you are standing on the path in front of it. The opening is just your height. You enter, standing quietly as you wait for your eyes to adjust to the sudden dimness.

Now you see that you are inside a perfect round cave. The air is warmer here; you can see the glowing embers of a fire in the center of the smooth floor, and smell the comforting smoky smell. On the walls around you are paintings that seem alive: animals run beside you, and people dance with horns or antlers on their heads. This cave feels good. You can feel the tension and anxiety draining away from you into the solid stone floor. You have come home.

You kneel beside the firepit and blow on the glowing embers until they flare into flame. You feed the fire with large branches piled nearby. Soon the cave walls glow warmly. In a niche in the smooth stone wall, you find dried fruit, seeds, a few succulent roots. The snow may come, but you will have warmth and food. You will be safe. You may want to imagine a clan of loving people there with you, or you may prefer to keep this cave for yourself alone. Know that you can come here in your mind whenever you need to feel secure. It is your inner cave of safety.

Seed-Thoughts on Earth as Sacred Stone

1. When we moved to upstate New York, my son, then seven, insisted on taking a large box of rocks with him. It seemed to weigh a ton (and we were paying for the move by the pound), but he couldn't bear to be parted from them. Some had interesting veins of quartz, others had fossils embedded in them, still others had fascinating shapes or colors, and some of them looked absolutely ordinary—but they were all special to him. He gets it honestly: special rocks are always appearing on my path asking to be treasured and honored, and some have had deep spirit-significance for me. At the end of a special workshop recently, we were invited to look for something in nature that we could pick up and keep as a talisman. I found a rock shaped like a bird in flight, which felt very right: I had begun a new life and felt that I was finally beginning to spread my wings.

   What are your stone-stories? If you don't do this already, begin to look for rocks that speak to you. Notice if you see the same shapes over and over (for years, it was a family joke that every rock I saw was either an owl or a primordial goddess). Some of us carry a special stone in our pockets to help soothe and ground us, a natural "worry stone" like the ones people have rubbed to release stress for ages. Some stones just feel so good in our hands. I have a special fondness for smooth, egg-shaped ones that fit perfectly in my palm. See what you can find.

2. In his later years, Carl Jung began to carve and build with stone. He wrote, "The stone has no uncertainties, no urge to communicate, and is eternally the same for thousands of years . . . this *was* the bottomless mystery of being, the embodiment of spirit." He allowed his intuition to dictate what gradually emerged on the famous Bollingen stone, placed just outside the door of his tower-

home in Switzerland. You may want to try your hand at carving or painting a special stone to be a marker or milestone for you. Find a stone that "speaks" to you, and see what you see on it. Jung first saw a small circle, like an eye, on the front of his. Allow yourself to be guided by your intuition. What wants to be expressed on the stone? Working with stone can be difficult, so using paints is an easier alternative than actually carving the rock, but you may feel called to get out a chisel and hammer. See what comes to you. Jung said, "When the stone was finished, I looked at it again and again, wondering about it and asking myself what lay behind my impulse to carve it." Lao Tzu says, "A good artist lets his intuition lead him wherever it wants."[9]

3. Are there any caves near you? You may want to make a pilgrimage to a nearby cave, just to have the experience of being surrounded by stone. Be sure to keep all your senses open if you go; later, you may want to write or draw your impressions. Can you describe the smell of rock? The texture of it as you touch it with your hand? What is the sound like in the middle of a cave? Do noises echo or become instantly absorbed in the stone? Can you see variations in the colors of the rock? How does it feel in your very soul to be standing in a cave? Look for seasonal activities taking place in caves in your area. One friend attended a predawn Winter Solstice celebration in a local cave. She told me, "It was one of the most powerful experiences I've ever had. There we were, huddling in this dark, hard place. It was really, really cold, and it seemed like the sun would never rise. But when it did, it shone right in through a hole in the cave roof. The light was so beautiful, the way it lit up the stone. It was incredible."

4. Look through old copies of National Geographic for photographs of mountains from different areas, in different seasons. Cut several of these pictures out, and spread them in front of you. Which one attracts you most? Choose one and really look at it. Now describe

it to yourself as fully and completely as you can. "My mountain is covered in green, very soft, surrounded by fields, rising up out of the fields gently." "My mountain is stony, jagged. The peak is covered in snow. The edges look sharp." "My mountain has streams and a waterfall pouring through it, cascading down it, very free-looking, very moist and beautiful." Now really listen to what you just said. Does this tell you anything about your life right now? About you? Your essential nature? This is a wonderful activity to try with friends. The way we see things is often the way we are. There is more to this exercise than meets the eye.

4

The Holy Garden Grove

I strayed down curving paths
past thickets, waist-high, where each
branch sang a different song of green
and flowers opened out in such brazen
and impenitent display that every bee was drunk
with nectar and delight.
O my garden, you have taught my feet
to wander closer to that
center where we will dance forever.

In a garden, we are surrounded by a natural beauty that is tamed just enough so that we feel safe. In a garden, with its lush fruits and fountains, we are never hungry or thirsty; we are taken care of. When we walk through the paradise garden, all our senses are charmed, engaged, lulled into a delicious state of pure enchantment. The paradise garden is an image of bliss that harks back, perhaps, to that paradise of our mother's womb or to the state of merged rapture we experienced in our mother's arms as she fed and cared for us. Certainly, gardens and the female body have been closely related in literature both secular and sacred for hundreds of years; just as earth is the maternal nourisher, a garden is the lush and fruitful embodiment of feminine delight.

A garden locked is my sister, my bride,
A garden locked, a fountain sealed.
Your shoots are an orchard of pomegranates
With all choicest fruits, henna with nard,
Nard and saffron, calamus and cinnamon,
With all trees of frankincense, myrrh and aloes, with all chief spices,
A garden fountain—a well of living water . . .
—SONG OF SOLOMON 4:12–15

The idea of a garden paradise is common to Muslims, Jews, and Christians; feminist scholar Barbara Walker has suggested that the Persian Pairidaeza (Paradise) was

> a magic garden surrounding the holy mountain of the gods, where the Tree of Life bore the fruit of immortality. Pairidaeza was also the divine Virgin who would give birth to the future Redeemer. . . . Shi'ite Muslims still look to the coming of the Virgin Paradise, the next Holy Mother. . . . The Hebrew *pardes*, "garden," was derived from the same Virgin Paradise.[1]

Sadly, as Joseph Campbell points out, "Christianity and Judaism are religions of exile: Man was thrown out of the Garden." There are many ways to understand this concept of the Fall, but certainly when people stopped believing in the sanctity of earth and our own spiritual oneness with it, they lost some vital capacity to connect with an essential source of joy. For some people, however, paradise was never lost but is ever-present in the earth around them, still attainable, found here and now; and it is still possible to experience the bliss of oneness with the Great Mystery. Here is a chant from the Navajo that expresses this merging with the One:

The mountains, I become part of it . . .
The herbs, the fir tree, I become part of it.

. . . .

The wilderness, the dew drops, the pollen . . .
I become part of it.[2]

For many people throughout history who believed in an immanent Mystery—and this includes many of our earliest ancestors—the
deepest experience of that Great Mystery was to be found in the
woods. Trees were sacred, and woods were places of worship. Sir James
Frazer tells us that the earliest Teutonic words for "temple" related to
natural woods. People throughout the wooded world have gathered in
groves to honor the spirits of the trees, and the goddesses and gods who
lived among them. For many centuries, the Celtic Druids, too, have
been associated with sacred groves, sites of many of their rituals. And
the ancient Greeks were no strangers to the sacred outdoor celebration, as the following scene from the poet Sappho shows:

In the young spring evening
The moon is shining full
Girls form a circle

. . . .

In the delicate flowering grass.[3]

Imagine walking in a dark wood at night, your path only barely
visible by the full moonlight glancing down through thick branches.
Ahead of you, you can see the flickering of a sacred fire, and you hear
the exciting heartbeat sound of many drums. Soon you break through
into a clear space, a circle of grass surrounded by a ring of trees, in the
center the fire ringed with stones, above you the moon circled by stars.
Around the fire are many people, all dancing and clapping, the drum-
beats and voices rising in a wild hymn praising the night, the moon,

the sacred trees, the Goddess of this grove. Imagine being welcomed by the spirit of this place. Imagine feeling one with it and with the others gathered here. Imagine the ecstasy of this oneness.

If the trees are sacred, then their wanton destruction is unthinkable. Many indigenous people believe that every species of tree and plant has its spirit, to which thanks must be offered. The Wanika of Eastern Africa equate destroying a coconut tree to matricide, since those trees give them nourishment and life, just as a mother nourishes her child. And many Buddhist monks will not break a branch of a tree, just as they would never break the arm of an innocent person. The forest is sacred in its aliveness, in its vibrant connection with the earth.

To rediscover a sense of oneness with nature, with the trees, is still within our reach. As Alice Walker wrote in *The Color Purple*, "One day when I was sitting quiet and feeling like a motherless child, which I was, it come to me: that feeling of being part of everything, not separate at all. I knew that if I cut a tree, my arm would bleed. And I laughed and I cried and I run all around the house." It is this very sensibility that moved activist Julia Butterfly Hill to live for more than two years in a giant California coast redwood tree to prevent its being cut down.

In "November Trees," from her book *Small Bird*, interfaith minister Elizabeth Cunningham compares the movement of treetrunks to the swaying of people reciting Jewish prayers.

In November when I see them
gathered grey, brown remnants
of leaf curling and wisping at their tips,
pooled in laps of root, the trees
look like their own ghosts
like lingering smoke, like incense
thick and sinuous. With the
green veil stripped away, I see

the whole trunk sways, as if
the trees are davening, these trees
who teach what temple columns are.[4]

Woods are wild and natural, but intentionally planted orchards
starred with blossoms and dropping with ripe fruit are to many people
lovely emblems of a lush and vital spirituality. The thirteenth-century
middle-Eastern poet Rumi wrote with passion of the "orchard where
the heart opens":

Come to the orchard in spring.
There is light and wine and
sweethearts in the pomegranate flowers.[5]

In the same century, Japanese Zen master Dogen, too, wrote beautifully of flowering fruit trees. His words evoke the simple grace of a
Japanese watercolor as he describes an old plum tree, "bent and
gnarled," opening first one blossom, then two, then three, then
uncountable blossoms:

not proud of purity,
not proud of fragrance;
spreading, becoming spring.[6]

And in the twentieth century, American beat poet and Buddhist
Kenneth Rexroth also wrote of an orchard as a place alive with spirit,
in words just as spare and immediate:

I sit under the old oak,
And gaze at the white orchard,
In bloom under the full moon.
The oak purrs like a lion,

And seems to quiver and breathe.
I am startled until I
Realize that the beehive
In the hollow trunk will be
Busy all night long tonight.[7]

So the image of the orchard has held a powerful resonance for these very different men, as it has for people throughout the world and in many different ages. Certainly, fruit tree blossoms have a scent that can only be described as heavenly, but any tree has about it something of the numinous. Like us, trees make a kind of bridge between earth and sky. Unlike us, they cannot run away. Patient and benign, they urge us to open our hearts and our senses, to experience the primal rapture of reconnection to our bodies, the beings that surround us, and this blessed, beautiful, and threatened planet.

The following activities invite you to get your hands dirty and to explore the sacred world of trees.

Spirit-Garden

This poem, with its amazingly contemporary voice, was actually written in the fourteenth century by the British nun Julian of Norwich:

Be a gardener.
Dig a ditch,
Toil and sweat,
And turn the earth upside down
And seek the deepness
And water the plants in time.[8]

Gardens bring us—immediately and vividly—into contact with the cycles and irrefutable laws of nature, teaching us indelible lessons about ourselves and about the messy, difficult, and beautiful processes of living. As Clarissa Pinkola Estés says,

> Sometimes, in order to bring a woman closer to the Life/Death/Life nature, I ask her to keep a garden. Let this be a psychic one or one with mud, dirt, green, and all the things that surround and help and assail. Let it represent the wild psyche. The garden is a concrete connection to life and death. You could even say that there is a religion of garden, for it teaches profound psychological and spiritual lessons. Whatever can happen to a garden can happen to soul and psyche—too much water, too little water, bugs, heat, storm, flood, invasion, miracles, dying back, coming back, boon, healing.[9]

So, I invite you to begin cultivating a garden. Anyone can do it: many city neighborhoods have community plots available, or you could join a community-supported agriculture project on a nearby farm, or plant something in a small window box. Spend some time intuiting what might want to be created through you. Are you longing for the colors and scents of flowers? Hungry for string beans? Herbs? Imagine.

When we garden with mindfulness, paying deep attention to all the many chores and pleasures of co-creating something with the earth, we deepen our connection to this sacred, powerful element. You may want to read Pam Montgomery's *Partner Earth* for a different perspective on what it means to be in true partnership with the planet.

Tree of Your Inner Spirit

This guided visualization is a way of accessing special information about yourself in the magical context of trees. Trees have much to teach us, and you don't have to be a tree expert or know any of the

Latin genus and species names to gather something of vital importance from them.

Sit comfortably with your eyes closed. Begin by noticing the sounds in the room around you. What are they? Take note of them. Now pay attention to the sounds your breathing makes as air enters your nostrils, then leaves them again. Just be with these small sounds that are your unique contribution to the noises in this place, right now.

Now begin to imagine walking in your favorite landscape on a beautiful day. Notice how the sky looks, the feeling of the earth under your feet. What does the air smell like? Feel like? Enjoy the bliss of walking in this lovely place.

Now you notice a tree rising up out of the ground ahead of you. Take special note of it. This tree has a spirit-kinship with you. What kind of tree is it? Is it evergreen or deciduous? Is it a graceful willow or a sturdy oak, a fragrant fir or something else entirely? What season is it in your tree? Does it have bright autumnal leaves, or tiny new spring ones? Is it bare and wintry, or lush in the fullness of summer? Does it bear any fruit or flowers? What is the trunk like? Is it smooth or furrowed? What is the weather like around your tree? Is there wind? Rain? Snow? Sunshine? Take note of everything about your tree. You may notice animals or birds in its branches.

Now approach your tree. You may want to lay your hand or cheek upon its trunk. This tree is filled with knowledge of you: it knows who you are and loves you all the same. This tree says something essential about the nature of your spirit. Spend some time with it. You may be moved to climb it, or to pluck and eat a piece of fruit from it, or pick a flower from it to wear in your hair.

Now thank the tree and turn away, knowing you can come back to see it any time. Bring your awareness back into this room, back to the sounds around you, back to the little noises your breathing makes as it enters your nostrils and leaves them again. Flex your fingers and toes, and open your eyes.

What kind of tree did you see? What do you know about it? Do some research if you like. When a client discovered her kinship with oak, she first gave some thought to oak's great sturdiness and beauty. Then she read up on oak trees and found out that they are sacred in many traditions, that they have age-old associations with abundance, and that, unlike most trees, they can be struck by lightning and survive. All this information was useful to her. She began to embrace her own sacred spirit-connection, her capacity to create abundance for herself, and her ability to survive trials by fire and emerge stronger than ever. Find pictures or photographs of your tree to place around your home where you will see them and be reminded.

Seed-Thoughts on Earth as Holy Garden Grove

1. What childhood memories do you have of gardens? When I was very small, my parents took me to a large public garden a few hours' drive from our home, and the experience has stayed with me all my life: the lush humid smell of the greenhouses, and the Grecian harmony of paths and urns and graceful plants, all fed something in me. What do you remember?

2. Imagine a garden of your dreams. Would it be stately or wild and tangled? What grows there? Are there fruit trees as well as flowers? Are there little winding paths or stately promenades? Secret bowers and nooks to sit in? Large sturdy trees to lean against? How does it smell? How do you feel when you go there in your mind? What does your spirit long for that this garden feeds?

   You may come across pictures that remind you of your spirit-garden. I recently opened a magazine to an article on a beautiful old house and organic garden in Provence that I somehow instantly recognized. "*This,*" I thought, "is it." It had soft, high banks of lush herbs, abundant fruit trees, a terrace where friends sat drinking wine in the setting sun surrounded by flowers—it looked like my idea of paradise. What does yours look like? You may want to begin collecting pictures from lifestyle and gardening magazines, not so you can deplete yourself and your bank account trying to replicate them, but just for dreaming, for soul-nourishment. Visit your spirit-garden often. Learn its paths and byways. You may discover things you didn't know were there: a secret spring, or a pool tucked away among the plants. Imagine picking a ripe apple from your spirit tree. Imagine how warm from the sun, how perfect and heavy it lies in your hand. Imagine its sweet scent, the lushness of its flavor. We can nourish ourselves so deeply with these images of the perfect garden: a ten-minute visit to it can feel better than a week-long vacation. Why wait? The fifteenth-century Indian poet Kabir says that inside our bodies there are flowers, and one flower has a thousand petals:

> That will do for a place to sit.
> Sitting there you will have a glimpse of beauty
> Inside the body and out of it,
> Before gardens and after gardens.[10]

3. We can find great comfort and pleasure when we engage in relationship with a particular tree in nature. As Philip Carr-Gomm says in *The Druid Tradition*, "Working with the spirit of the tree can bring us renewed energy, powerful inspiration and deep communion."

   Many of us have had trees in our lives that were special to us. I once loved a magnificent oak with three trunks that stood at a crossroads in the woods where three deer-paths converged. I called her the Hecate Tree, after the triple-headed goddess of the crossroads, and brought her little offering gifts of pomegranates, which the squirrels happily pillaged. Although I am unable to visit her now, she remains safe in my heart forever. What trees have been special to you? Were there trees you climbed as a child? A tree that grew outside your apartment in the city? Think back.

All of us need a tree to love. Trees are as unique and individual as people, and those of us who spend time with them come to sense and honor their singular presence. If you have trees growing near you, go and introduce yourself, or take a drive to a nearby park or wild area to find one that feels right to you. Spend some time simply sitting beside your tree. Trees make wonderful companions. Sit with your back against it, if you like, or lie down at its roots and look up at its branches. Get to know your tree in all seasons, in all weathers. You may want to name your tree and leave small gifts for it: trees often need water or fertilizer, but I have been told that they appreciate other things as well—crystals, shells, locks of hair. It is an honor to be known as a tree-hugger: wrap your arms around your tree and join the clan! Some of us just love to touch our trees, and the feeling of bark under our hands is so grounding and soothing. What does the *spirit* of your tree feel like? A willow will feel quite different to you than a yew. Once you have formed a relationship with your tree, it becomes a true friend in times of trouble, willing to give solace and comfort in its wordless but very powerful way.

4. Walking in the woods can be a deeply spiritual experience. A special peace descends on us when we give ourselves over to being in a woods, simply looking, listening, smelling, feeling. Such an abundance of life is there that we can't help but be touched by it, and feel ourselves part of it, in a way that goes very deep. Do you have any woods that are special to you? Take time as often as you can to visit them. If you live far from forests, look for pictures or photographs that will give you a sense of that sacred wild, green energy. You may find that you begin to visit the woods in your dreams.

Water

Introducing Water

God rises up out of the sea like a treasure in the waves.
—THOMAS MERTON

We stand at night beside a vast body of water, its surface rising and falling like the breathing of some huge beast. We smell the sharp salty richness of its breath; our ears are filled with its song, the muffled roar of inexorable advance and retreat, foam and gritty sand, treasures and trash thrust onto the shore with every wave, then gradually dragged back into the depths again. In its belly, we know, are creatures in multitudes beyond our comprehension. As the full moon rises the water stretched out before us gleams—and we feel a tremendous pull and power.

Both our planet and our bodies are made mostly of water, subject to tides and cycles, rhythmic patterns of breath and heartbeat and flow. Water is vital to us, our need for it both explicit and sharply imperative: without it, in just a few short days we die. Although technology has changed our world in ways that our ancestors could never understand, we ourselves—our basic nature and spirit—have changed very little. When we begin to swim with Water, exploring it and tasting its fundamental spiritual power, we reconnect with the very essence of being human.

What do we know about the essential nature of water? It is, after all, a slippery element, hard to pin down unless it falls under the spell of bitter cold that turns it to solid ice. It takes on the shape of whatever contains it in the moment, constantly shifting and changing, so we often understand water as an emblem for emotions, likewise mutable. When we are in the depths of great feeling, the going can be very slow and heavy, like trying to move underwater. And emotion often manifests in watery tears, whose salinity reminds us of our beginnings in the sea. Like love, water cannot be held in a clenched fist, only in a cupped hand; water seems to speak a language of the heart.

Water as emotion, though, is only a drop in the proverbial bucket. Throughout history, people have understood water as a teacher of the mysteries of life, death, and rebirth. And in most major world religions, water is the great purifier that cleanses us of all that obscures our true light. Water is also the compassionate healer, relieving thirsts both actual and metaphorical. And water has age-old associations with numinous Source: wells, pools, and springs, particularly, are associated with magic and spirit-based creativity. Water, then, holds a rich and mysterious broth of spiritual attributes understood by people everywhere: the mystery of life/death/life, the power of purification, the healing balm of compassion, and the mystical presence of creative magic.

Water invites us to dive into a personal connection with its immensity. We begin by exploring how it is understood and celebrated the world over, and then we can navigate our own way, using simple, powerful tools rooted in the great spiritual traditions that still leave plenty of room for our own unique, deep knowing.

Water Prayer

Great wetness:
The beat of your waves is the beat of my breathing;
the surge of your tides is the surge of my heart.
My very cells pray to you; my tears, sweat, and blood sing your song.
Without you, I wither and die.

Teach me your secrets of ebbing and flowing,
help me to trust in your pattern repeating.
Buoy me up, teach me to swim in you,
help me to rest in your arms.

5

The Great Maternal Sea

We first know water as the sunless sea of our mother's womb: something in our very cells remembers the sensation of drifting on that dark, warm current of amniotic fluid. Our individual watery beginnings are microcosms for the origins of life on this planet, in the oceans where simple life-forms appeared, proliferated, and became increasingly complex—until some of them washed up on land and survived. So it is no surprise that humans all over the world find a common watery ground in creation myths that begin with an endless maternal sea, a chaos of watery formlessness out of which earth and matter arise. The human spirit understands water as the Great Beginning.

Many Native American creation stories—in place long before the influence of Christian missionaries—bear an uncanny resemblance to the account in Hebrew Scripture. For instance, a Hopi creation myth starts, "In the beginning, the earth was nothing but water." And in their "Song of the World," the Pima Indians of Arizona say, "In the beginning there was only darkness everywhere—darkness and water." Compare with the biblical Genesis: "The earth was without form and void, and darkness was upon the face of the deep; and the Spirit of God was moving over the face of the waters."

Feminist scholar Barbara Walker, in her *Woman's Encyclopedia of Myths and Secrets*, suggests that the Aramaic word for the "deep," *tehom*, derives from the Babylonian primordial goddess Tiamat, related to the Egyptian Temu, mother of water, darkness, and night. Tiamat and Temu are only two of legions of ancient oceanic creation goddesses, from the Sumerian Nammu to the Peruvian Mama Cocha, whose name means "Mother Sea," to the Micronesian Liomarar, who created islands by throwing sand around in the great void of her water. The Tlingit Indians of the Pacific Northwest, who rely on the ocean for every aspect of life, have given it a thousand names: to them, as to many indigenous people, the sea is Mother.

When we look at the earliest roots of world religions, water is often fundamental. The ancient Hindus believed the sky was made of water, the upper part of a great cosmic ocean. Hindu mythology evolved later into the concept of the goddess Maha-Kali, the Great Power, an ocean of womb-blood out of which all four elements arose. For Muslims, too, water was primal; the sixth-century Arab historian Masudi relates that in Islamic cosmology, water was the first thing God created. And the Hebrews also honored water in their way: the mighty temple of Solomon contained a huge basin representing the Mother Sea (1 Kings 7:23).

But, like fire, the other "wild" or powerful element, water is destroyer as well as creator, feared as well as revered. The biblical flood story is a graphic account of global annihilation through water: "And the water prevailed so mightily upon the earth that all the high mountains under the whole heaven were covered. . . . And all flesh died that moved upon the earth, birds, cattle, beasts, all swarming creatures that swarm upon the earth, and every man; everything on the dry land in whose nostrils was the breath of life died" (Genesis 7:19–22).

Throughout the world, in art as well as in religion, the ocean is inextricably linked with death. Aristotle believed that no creature could die except when the tide was ebbing. According to Sir James Frazer's *The Golden Bough*, this belief persisted all up and down the European coast for centuries. Dickens echoes it in *David Copperfield*, when Peggotty says, "People can't die, along the coast, except when the tide's pretty nigh out." The Haida people of the Pacific Northwest say that someone who is about to die sees a canoe manned by dead friends, who say, "Come with us now, for the tide is about to ebb and we must depart."

Ebbing tides are not the only ocean aspect that evokes death. For Shakespeare, in his Sonnet 60, the waves themselves sing of life's terrible brevity:

Like as the waves make to the pebbled shore,
So do our minutes hasten to their end,
Each changing place with that which goes before,
In sequent toil all forwards do contend. . . .

The chaotic and formidable nature of water has been celebrated in literature throughout the ages; we voyage upon it with Homer's Odysseus, battle its monsters with Melville's Ahab, and learn its secrets with Annie Proulx's Quoyle. The ocean, with its seemingly endless and savage beauty, becomes a symbol for anything that is larger than individual human life, unpredictable and potentially fatal. For John Millington Synge, in his great Irish play *Riders to the Sea*, it is War, ripping away the young men of the village in multitudes.

Certainly, humans are deeply aware of the sea's frightening potential for danger. To seafaring people worldwide, with their generations of the drowned, the ocean can be a great, fierce cauldron where eater and eaten are at last boiled down together, an untamed and untamable presence. Seaside-dwelling indigenous people have long sought to appease and control the implacable force of water with ritual offerings and ceremony, but, despite all human attempts at control and intervention, the sea remains, like deity, a Mystery. The Yoruba have a proverb that sums it up succinctly: "Nobody knows what's at the bottom of the Ocean."

All things arise from water, the First Mother, and return to her, the Great Destroyer, but she offers rebirth, as well. For millennia, water, particularly rivers, with their ceaseless flow in one direction, has taught humanity valuable lessons about the nature of time and of existence itself: constantly changing, forever new and yet the same, an emblem of eternal life. It is no wonder, then, that water in its river form has age-old associations with resurrection—from the River Styx, watery route to the land of death and rebirth, to the River Jordan, once thought to possess the ability to "remake one's flesh into that of a little child" (2 Kings 5:14). Those who lived by the sea understood that water burials—where the dead are placed in ships or rafts and set adrift in the current—were a return to the Beginning.

Today, many people go to certified rebirthers, immersing themselves in vats of warm, salinated water to heal the ill effects of difficult in-utero or birth experiences, or they visit sensory deprivation tanks to experience the utter relaxation of a dark, wet, womblike environment.

I have noticed in my counseling practice, as well as in my own life, that our relationship with our mother is often reflected in our attitudes toward large bodies of water. To give a personal example, after a lifetime of uneasiness toward the ocean, I recently had a transformative dream, probably the fruit of several years of working through issues around my own beloved mother. In the dream I was swimming in the sea at night, when I realized I was lost—I couldn't tell which way was land, which was the far horizon—and then I made the choice to simply relax and trust the current, which eventually carried me in to shore. Now I'm planning a trip to the ocean, knowing I will probably perceive it in a very different way.

To create a personal experience of the great life/death/life nature of water, bathing is the activity of choice. When approached with consciousness, a bath can be a kind of rebirth, a making-new of self.

Bath of Form and Formlessness

Find a time after dark when you will not be disturbed. Turn off the phone and the bathroom lights, and light a candle to provide just enough illumination for safety. Run a warm, deep bath, and add at least one cup of sea salt. (Sea salt is preferable over the commercial kind because it is usually less processed and because it comes directly from the sea, which is what we're trying to replicate here. You can find it at your local natural food store.) Now immerse yourself in the tub, and close your eyes.

Imagine that your body is dissolving into the water along with the salt. Just a moment ago, the grains were hard and angular; now they are as silky and smooth as the water, permeating every drop. Imagine the peace of being present but in a different form—a changing, mutable form. Imagine that this dark tub filled with water and salt is a great ocean, glimmering with stars. Allow yourself to breathe gently like the sea, rising and falling with its gentle, primal rhythm. You are a vast cauldron filled with essential life-stuff, the nourishing broth of ages, rich and thick with possibility. Experience the rhythm of heart and breath as waves, gently ebbing and flowing. Know that your blood, your body's fluids carry the memory of Ocean, their salinity the same as the sea. Know that you are the child of this vast mother. Allow yourself to be rocked by her. Imagine releasing any old hurts that burden or distress you into these great maternal arms.

Now imagine that you are beginning to coalesce, to re-form—still as yourself, but new. Imagine your bones taking shape as conduits of light out of the warm darkness—hollow, healthy, and gleaming. Imagine strong muscles draping themselves beautifully over and around those bones and imagine organs, glistening and perfect, packing themselves inside the spaces between the bones. As they take shape, imagine the perfection of every cell of your body, glowing like a trillion moons in the dark water. Imagine the beauty of your skin, your hair, the unique features of your face.

Now you are whole. Make your rising out of the water a dedication to beginning anew.

By the power of Water, I am reborn.
May my actions proceed from Water's grace,
my thoughts from the memory of oneness with her.
May I glow in this ocean of souls like a star,
one drop among many, uniquely myself.

Give yourself time to be quiet and restful after you are dry; the newly born often need to sleep. Be kind to your new self.

This second activity is based on cross-cultural water-burial traditions that have been practiced unchanged since before the beginnings of recorded time. It may seem simple, but it contains a surprising depth and capacity to move and transform.

Grieving with Water

Just a few days after the World Trade Center disaster, still in shock, fear, and grief, a friend and I went down to a gentle shore of the Hudson River, north of New York City. We found a piece of birchbark on the ground and took turns writing a prayer on its smooth inner surface. We put a dried rosebud on the bark, placed this bundle on the river, and watched it slowly float downstream toward the place where so many mourned. We sang as we watched it disappear, our voices rough and unsteady. But when we finally turned away to go home, we felt more deeply at peace.

Water gives us a way to honor our mourning over the loss of something dear to us. When we place our grief in Water's arms, she will hold it for us.

Write something that you are mourning on a piece of bark (preferably found on the ground, not removed from a tree) and place it on the surface of a river or stream where the current can carry it away. You may want to pray or sing as you watch it travel out of sight. If feelings come up, let them flow. People have offered their dead to water in just this way for millennia, knowing that she is large enough to hold it all. Now take a deep breath, and turn back toward the rest of your life.

The following are some questions for meditation; simply moodling about with them may lead you deeper into your own understanding of water in its life/death/life aspect. Water, as we know, makes a fine mirror. For many centuries, people have used it thus, not only to see their own reflections but to see life reflected in a mysterious and oblique way that can be very enriching.

Reflections on Water as the Mystery of Life/Death/Life

1. What were the circumstances surrounding your own gestation? Your birth? Ask your mother if she is still alive, or others who may know the answers.

2. What is your very first memory of water?

3. Re-create a sense-memory of a pleasant childhood experience of water. What were the sights, smells, textures, sounds surrounding you?

4. Visit a body of water that moves—an ocean, river, or stream. Just be there, listening, watching, smelling, feeling. Spending time beside water is a form of prayer, a way of knowing the Divine Mystery in its fluid form. What emotions arise in you as you experience this moving water? The details that we notice often give us clues about our own inner nature. What do you see?

5. Spend time beside a still body of water—a lake or pond. Simply be there, listening, watching, smelling, feeling. What is this experience like for you? Do you feel differently than you did when the water beside you moved? What details do you notice? What do they tell you about your own essential watery nature? How do you sense the spirit-presence of still water?

6. What are your own personal feelings toward the ocean? Large rivers? Lakes? What is your favorite body of water? Describe it in

as much detail as you can. For example, I love the Hudson River. I might write, "It is calm and powerful. It flows with great strength and determination. It embraces the rocks; it nourishes the roots of many trees. It sings a gentle song." Now imagine that you have just written a description of yourself. Can you accept this way of understanding your own water-nature?

7. If you could imagine a boat to live on, what would it be like? Boats are universal symbols for the means by which we navigate the vast waters of our lives. Is your boat sturdy? Sleek? Simple? Decorative? Look in magazines (*National Geographic* is ideal) and find pictures of boats that feel right to you. Cut them out and place them where you can see them and be reminded of your own navigational ability.

8. What is water's significance for you? One dear friend amusingly relates that turning points in her life are often accompanied by water. The day she met her Quigong master, an open water-cooler spigot created a small flood on the floor at her feet. After her Third Degree Reiki attunement, she accidentally sat on a bottle of water, which burst and soaked her to the skin. What stories do you tell about water?

6

The Universal Solvent

May the gentleness of spring rains
Soften the tensions within us.
—Janet Schaffran and Pat Kozak[1]

W̱ater's power to purify and renew is a strange and very beautiful
phenomenon. Every year the spring rains fall, and winter's gray
snow, the patches of dead grass obscured by dust, are bathed and transformed; the world emerges clean and sparkling with life. Or think of a
woman in deep mourning: her sorrow lies like a rock in the center of her
chest. But when she is finally able to cry, her tears seem to wash away a
little of her heaviness. She experiences an easing, a feeling of relief.

Since the very dawn of human time, people have marveled at water's
ability to cleanse, to make fresh. When I began thinking about water as
purifier, I remembered my father, a chemical engineer, telling me that
water is known as the universal solvent. I started to wonder about the
relationship between the words "solvent" and "absolve." I looked to
Webster's for answers and found "solvent" (from the Latin *solvere*, to dissolve, to loosen) defined as "something that eliminates or attenuates
something esp. unwanted; something that provides a solution."
"Absolve" means "to set free from an obligation or the consequences of

guilt; to remit a sin by absolution." Solvent, dissolving, solution, absolution: all this wordplay is a sort of linguistic reminder that water, in many world religions, is ritually used to take away sins.

When we consider the adage "Cleanliness is next to godliness," we're really seeing a variation on an ancient theme of spiritual purity versus spiritual uncleanness. In the age-old fight against impurity, water is on the side of the angels. Even in spiritual paths with no lexicon of duality and no concept of uncleanness or sin, water offers a way of starting fresh, an initiation into new ways of being, of letting go of any actions, memories, or habits that impede progress or that have taken the self away from its natural connection with Mystery.

Since the beginning of time, people have washed themselves not only to remove dirt or sin but to cleanse themselves from something too big, too sacred, or too powerful for humans to bear. Many tribal religions practice washing to remove "taboo," a word that has come to mean "forbidden" but that originally meant "sacred." In *The Golden Bough*, Sir James Frazer tells us that washing after contact with something is a sign that the object touched possessed magical, sacred, or supernatural powers. So the ancient Egyptian practice of washing after touching pigs—sacramental animals that were sacrificed and eaten once a year—argues for the sacredness of pigs. The ancient Greeks washed both their clothes and their bodies in a river or stream before they could return home after making an expiatory sacrifice; their contact with the sacred nature of the sacrifice was just too potent for daily life. And the ancient Jews washed their hands after reading the sacred scriptures.

Every human being understands the link between water and cleansing; it is a deep knowing that crosses religious and cultural boundaries, a truth of the inner spirit. As Clarissa Pinkola Estés points out in *Women Who Run with the Wolves*, "To wash something is a timeless purification ritual. It not only means to purify, it also means—like baptism from the Latin *baptiza*—to drench, to permeate with a spiritual numen and mystery." Renewal of soul happens in the water.

Christian baptism is a watery purification rite that echoes this idea of spiritual rebirth. It also embodies the idea of the great maternal sea we visited in the previous chapter. Erich Neumann points out in *The Great Mother* that during the Catholic ritual of consecration of the baptismal font, when a burning candle is about to be dropped into the water, the font is referred to by the celebrant in Latin as an *immaculato utero,* a "stainless womb."

Jesus' cousin John the Baptist offered followers immersion in the River Jordan in the spirit of repentance after they had confessed their sins (Matthew 3:4); Jesus himself was one of the first to be baptized in this way. (It is interesting to note that despite a lack of any biblical evidence, tradition has it that John used a clamshell to baptize Jesus, hence the clamshell motif on many Catholic baptismal fonts. When we appreciate the very female shape of the clamshell, this could be seen as another reemergence of the ancient maternal aspect of water.)

The relationship between water and purification was already firmly in place in Jesus' day. Ancient Jewish practices included no fewer than four different purification rites involving water. The first involved cleansing as preparation for initiation—to a higher order of the priesthood, for example. Another rite was part of readying oneself to perform specific religious rituals: ancient Hebrew priests had to wash their hands and feet before approaching the altar, on pain of death. A third type was the *mikvah,* a ritual usually performed by women after each monthly flow for the purpose of shedding the "uncleanness" associated with menstrual blood—a substance that was once revered in virtually every ancient culture. (Anita Diamant's *The Red Tent,* a work of historical fiction, revolves around the sacredness of a woman's monthly bleeding time as celebrated by the ancient Jewish people. This corroborates Sir James Frazer's idea that if you have to wash after contact with something, it's probably sacred.) The fourth purification rite cleansed the participant from guilt; when Pilate washed his hands to prove his innocence of Jesus' blood (Matthew 27:24), he was performing a ritual the Jewish people would understand.

Muslims developed their own highly complex purification practices, the *ghusi*, for example—a ritual washing of the entire body in ceremonially pure water for the purpose of cleansing the soul from defilement. Many Muslim landscapes are notoriously arid; water is scarce. We can only imagine the lengths to which penitents would have to go in order to gather enough water for this ritual.

Like Jews and Muslims, Hindus have practiced immersion to wash away sin for millennia. It is said that the greatly revered River Ganges, named for the Hindu goddess Ganga, has waters so potent that even a breeze charged with its vapor can erase the accumulated sins of a million lifetimes. Belief in this power continues unabated; multitudes still throng to its shores every year to bathe, to be made new. It is considered a special blessing on the dead for the corpse to be dipped in its sacred waters before cremation. Other Indian rivers are also considered holy because it is believed that they are linked underground to the Ganges.

Swami Saradananda, yoga teacher and author, describes her Ganges experience:

> In India, where all rivers are sacred, water symbolizes purification on a physical as well as a much deeper level. I remember this every time I trek to Gomukh, the source of the Ganges River. Here the heavenly Ganga emerges from her Himalayan cave to begin Her journey on Earth. As I plunge into the bone-freezing waters, I feel at one with Her, sins are washed away, my mind is pure and clear, and I understand why, to the Hindu mind, water is equated with the divine flow of consciousness.

Daily bathing, too, is used by many faiths as a ritual purification, cleansing the inner self as well as the outer body. The ancient Greeks and Romans may have bathed mainly for comfort and simple cleanliness, but the ancient Egyptians believed that washing was a spiritual activity. Egyptian priests bathed in cold water twice a day and twice every night; this, along with ritually shaving the entire body every third day, was thought to promote purity of soul.

For devout Hindus, the daily ritual bath is accompanied by a prayer invoking the goddess Ganga. In this way, any container of water becomes charged with Ganga's spiritual cleansing power. Followers of Islam also practice daily water rites that go beyond simple notions of personal hygiene. Muslim prayers are performed five times a day, and they must be preceded by the *wudu*, or ceremonial washing, a vital part of the preparation process. To facilitate this, most mosques include little cubicles, complete with basins and towels, for their celebrants to use.

Those of us who follow a more eclectic path can also use ritual bathing to good effect. Elizabeth Cunningham, novelist, poet, and interfaith minister, reports that she takes different kinds of baths depending on what she needs. "I have a bathtub altar," she says, "with candles, and images of the snake goddess, shells, rocks. There's a window next to my bathtub, and sometimes I take moon baths, charging my bathwater with moonlight, or I take candlelit baths. Or I'll take a Dark Bath, when I really need to dissolve, go into the deep places, to let go of the little hamster-wheel thoughts. I've found that it can really help."

Ritual bathing is also a part of some Buddhist practices, although with a slightly different twist. In China and Japan, devotees bathe statues of the Buddha with water or tea on his birthday, celebrated on the eighth day of the fourth month. The custom re-creates the magical bath that the baby Buddha is said to have been given by heavenly beings at his birth as a proof of his divine purity.

Tibetan Buddhists use a water purification ritual to prepare for the Chenresig Empowerment. Chenresig, also spelled Chenresi or Chenreysik, is the Tibetan name for Avalokiteshvara, the famous bodhisattva of universal compassion. The goal of the empowerment is for participants to replace their ordinary identity with that of Chenresig.

As described by Robert Thurman, "The Lama has prepared himself, and the disciples must prepare as well. After touching each student on the head with the Action vase, the Lama pours consecrated water from the vase into their hands. They rinse their mouths with the water to symbolize their leaving behind ordinary habits of perception as they enter the ritual space."[2] I have found photographs of this ritual very beautiful; the act of cupping the hands and bringing the water to one's mouth seems very basic and profound.

It is interesting to note that for Christians, spiritual purification by water is a once-in-a-lifetime experience, whereas other religions developed an ongoing, often daily cleansing practice. It must be stated here that many early Christians were actively suspicious of bodily cleanliness, associating it with the voluptuous excesses of Rome and its famous baths. This prejudice persisted for centuries; the Crusaders, for example, were noticeably filthy, especially in comparison to the oft-washed Muslims they encountered.

Among some indigenous people, ritual washing marks the closure of one way of life and a rebirth into the new one; in this way it is not unlike the Christian baptism that is a rebirth into the family of Christ. For example, a special bath or ceremonial hair-washing is considered part of a young woman's coming-of-age ritual by many Navajo people, although there is no implication of sin that needs to be cleansed away.

Purification with water often plays an important role for spiritually conscious hands-on healers, such as Reiki practitioners, who usually incorporate hand-washing at the end of a session to clear away any unwanted energies. Those who work with crystals in their healing practice often soak the stones in salt water periodically to cleanse and recharge them. And a friend says that she often steps across running water when she needs to release some negative feeling or memory. "Once," she confides, "I needed to break the curse of my father's words to me. I made a ritual of breaking a dry stick in two pieces and giving them to the stream, letting the water carry them away."

Small amounts of water are used in many traditions to purify, bless, or consecrate. Wiccans, for example, often use salt water to prepare their magical tools as well as to cast the circle of purification and protection before ritual work. Many witches also cast a salt water circle around their homes on Samhain, the ancient holy day now known as Halloween, when it is believed that the veil between the worlds is thin and spirits of the departed come back for a little visit. The salt water circle can be seen as a sort of spiritual housecleaning and also as a way to keep all but the invited spirit-guests away. Women have used herbs and oils in their housecleaning water for centuries to combat negativity as well as grime. (For some ideas on magical housekeeping, see my handbook on restoring a sense of Spirit to cooking and eating, *Witch in the Kitchen: Magical Cooking for All Seasons*.) Similarly, Catholic priests also mix water with other substances—wine, ashes, and salt, for example—to be used in the consecration of altars and churches. And we also find holy water in small basins at the entryways of every Roman Catholic church, used to invoke God's presence, ward off evil, and cleanse the inner self.

Many earth-honoring people believe that *all* water is holy, worthy of being treated with the utmost respect and reverence. Open your heart to the mystery of water, that sacred substance so essential to human life, and polluting it will be a sacrilege. Open your heart to its preciousness, and you will be less likely to waste it. We cannot live without it, and yet in many places the water is poisoned or terribly scarce. When we truly realize both how necessary and how blessed water is, then our interactions with it become more mindful.

The following simple purification rituals invite us to bathe in the hope of beginning again, free of the past's deadening debris. Water may feel gentle and soft, but it is strong enough to cut deep channels in rock, to smooth jagged stones. It is strong enough to ease your heart; it is your ally in starting fresh.

Here is a marvelous poem to help get you into a watery frame of mind. You will notice that it is shaped, evocatively, like a fish:

A mermaid dives deep.
She is not afraid of
what may be buried at the
bottom of her fluid heart.
She is not frozen in fear
watching from the dunes.
Instead a mermaid swims the waters
where she bathes in her own
self love.

To be a sea-maid, one must breathe
with the wisdom that freedom
is not walking the shore, but
touching bottom with faith
that one rebounds to fresh waters,
through open eyes, with clear lungs,
a willing heart, and new skin
to breath out the old,
and in the daring.

A mermaid knows
memory is both
a chain that binds,
and the key that frees;
And
the truth that heals
in the name of The Mother,
The Daughter, and The Holy Self.
Amen.

—IRENE YOUNG[3]

The Well of Releasing

Make a little private time for yourself. You are about to create a numinous well, a place where you can release old hurts and regrets and find renewal. This sacred well is the place of letting go and refilling, where the soul-self can find both relief and solace.

Find a large bowl, basin, or stockpot and fill it with fresh water. You may want to sprinkle in a tiny bit of sea salt and some fresh or dried herbs; thyme and sage are both wise choices for purification. Place the well on a countertop or table, turn off the lights, and light a candle. Stand for a few moments looking into your well. Remember how the molecules of this water have evaporated, rising up from the earth, then coalesced into clouds and fallen as rain or as snow on distant mountains, melted as springs, flowed over and under the earth, collected in pools, lakes, and rivers, then evaporated again, then fallen, then reformed, in an eternal cycle as old as the planet. Any water partakes of the essence of Water. So it is with your well. It is connected to sacred waters everywhere.

Now give some thought to something you want to release: an old hurt, a damaging memory, a self-limiting pattern of behavior, an isolating or imprisoning habit. Plunge your hands into the water. Now wash them, visualizing all these things washing away, being released, purified by the power of water, leaving you free and clear.

Raise your hands up out of the well now, and watch the drops falling back like stars. Rub your hands together to dry them. Thank the water. Be sure to empty your well in a mindful way—using it to water your plants, perhaps. As you watch them thrive you will be reminded of the ways in which your old "stuff" can be used for growth.

Washing Away Fear

When we name our fears, they lose some of their power to make us freeze, shut down, give up. Add the magic of water—the solvent that dissolves what is unwanted—and we have the makings of a simple but highly effective ritual.

You will need water-soluble pastels (available at craft or art supply stores, and well worth the trip; the colors are rich and saturated and they wash off with ease, a real necessity for this activity), a basin of water, and a washcloth. Find a safe, quiet place. You may play some soothing music if you like. Now gently bring your awareness to what frightens you. What do you dread? Death? Poverty? Being seen? *Not* being seen? Failing? Succeeding? Being alone? Being with the wrong person? There is no end to the things we have to fear. What fears haunt you? Find a color in your box of pastels that feels right to you, and write your own particular fear somewhere on your body. See it named. You may write as many fears as you need.

Now take the cloth, immerse it in the water, wring it out, and gently wipe away your fear. Rinse out the cloth; see how the water takes on the color of your fear. Imagine that the water has taken your fear away from you. When you are finished and washed clean of your fear-words, take the basin outside and pour the water out onto the earth. Watch how it is absorbed. The elements are large enough to contain and transform your fears.

One chilly autumn night, several of us met in the renovated barn that is our alternative community center of choice and performed this as a ritual together by candlelight. Gigi, the woman who brought this idea to the group, lay down on a sheet in the center of our circle, and we wrote our fears on her arms, her legs, her face, her belly. Then we took turns washing each other's fears away. What a magical evening it was! You may want to share this idea with a few trusted friends. Spirit-acts performed in community are empowering, encouraging, and a lot of sacred fun.

Reflections on Water as Purifier

1. What memories do you have of bathing? Most of us shower now, but when we were children, we were bathed. Like many of you, I

suspect, I was a little wild child who spent my childhood summers getting dirty and sticky playing in the woods. Then evening would fall, and I would come in for my bath. My mother bought me sweet-smelling bubble bath, talcum powder, and a special cologne for little girls called "rose-mint." I emerged from the tub in a dense fog of scent. But I still remember the peace of lying in bed, no longer itchy and sweaty but clean, smooth, and ready for sleep. What do you remember?

2. Have you ever gone skinny-dipping? How was it different from swimming clothed? How did your body feel when you were in the water? When you emerged? There is sometimes a tremendous innocence and playfulness in swimming naked—a return to child-like purity. You may want to pick a nice, hot day and a safe place, and try it.

3. Most of us are burdened by shame. For some of us, simply being female is enough to make us feel less-than, especially if we grew up in patriarchal religions that taught the inferiority of women, that made us see ourselves as tainted with sin and pollution and blamed for the fall of mankind. Even if we were fortunate enough to escape this damning heritage, our culture shames us with impossible ideals of female beauty that none of us can hope to attain, as the means of promoting multi–billion-dollar beauty and weight-loss industries. Now imagine what it would be like to be shame-free. Imagine bathing in a great pool where shame is dissolved away. Imagine rising out of the water like a goddess, free to be powerful and truly beautiful in your own unique way. Write a description of this, using the present tense: "I rise up from the water, fully alive, big-bellied and unashamed, free to stand tall, powerful and strong." Share this idea with your friends. What would it be like if we could dissolve our shame away together?

7

The Compassionate Healer

Now we come to water in its role as Compassionate One, the reliever of thirst, the numinous presence who fills us with healing. But water still retains its Great Maternal aspect here: healing renews life. And in taking away disease, water is still the Purifier as well. We can try to understand water by separating its characteristics into chapters, but the element itself delights in aiming a big splash at such arbitrary divisions. After all, where do we really draw the line between purification and healing? Between rebirth and healing? How can we draw any line at all in water, anyway? It simply *is*: interpenetrating, flowing back and forth and through. Each aspect of water is present in every other; ultimately, it will refuse to be contained. Perhaps most importantly, in this chapter water becomes our teacher about the falseness of another kind of division: that between body, mind, and spirit. To water, all is one. All dis-ease is one. All healing is one. Water connects us, linking feeling and thought and sensation, like the fluid that fills each cell and runs through every vein. The thirsty body and the thirsty soul mirror each other. The same element heals them both.

Real thirst is almost outmoded now. Many of us tote bottles of water around with us wherever we go, sipping whenever the thought crosses our minds, whether we feel thirsty or not. But if you have ever been truly parched—really desperate for moisture—and then have been given a drink, you know what it is to feel grateful for water, for its gift of easing thirst. It makes deep spirit-sense that water is an emblem of compassion, perhaps especially among desert people. And for humans everywhere, water is often a fitting image for the Great Spirit that both comforts and heals.

People associate "taking the waters" with healing; spas and springs have been refuges of the afflicted for millennia. (My husband and I spent our honeymoon—at the tender age of twenty-one—in Berkeley Springs, West Virginia, after reading an enthusiastic blurb in *Country Inns and Back Roads*. What that book didn't tell us was that we would be sharing our romantic inn with scores of elderly people in wheelchairs and walkers, surrounded by the rotten-egg smell of the sulfur springs. It was not the most fortuitous beginning for a marriage.)

The ancient Romans were famous for building spas and healing resorts wherever they marched. Bath, in England, is a well-known example. Bath was originally the shrine of Sulis (whose name means "sun"), a Celtic goddess of healing whom the Romans identified with their own goddess Minerva; she presided over the only hot springs known in England. To the Romans, homesick for the warmth of their native climate, Bath was undoubtedly a source of great relief from English damp and chill. People have sought healing and rejuvenation in Bath for centuries, and references to it abound in literature, from Chaucer, with his Wife of Bath, to Jane Austen and Charles Dickens, who both had residences there.

The Romans did not bring the idea of sacred springs to the British Isles, however; the Celts had long considered water and healing to be inextricably twined. Celtic mythology teems with wells, pools, and springs believed to have both indwelling spirits and curative properties; the water itself is sacred. There are countless stories about pools of wisdom, springs of healing, and rivers of transformation, which were once magical Pagan sites sacred to various gods and goddesses but were later given saints' names by the Christians. This fragment, for instance, concerns the Welsh Saint Gwenfrewi, who was once, probably, a much older water deity.

> Where her head was lifted, a spring was found . . .
> Healing for every disease is within it . . .
> Making body and soul whole.[1]

Like the Celts, the ancient Greeks believed that bodies of water had magical inhabitants, some of whom were called Naiads. Here the poet Dr. John Armstrong celebrates this idea in "The Art of Preserving Health," written supposedly under the inspiration of Hygeia, the Roman goddess of healing (from whence came our word "hygiene").

> Come, ye Naiads! To the fountains lead!
> O comfortable streams! With eager lips
> And trembling hands the languid thirsty quaff
> New life in you; fresh vigor fills their veins.[2]

An emphasis on the sacred healing properties of water is found in the New World as well. The ancient Aztecs worshipped a watery goddess, Teteu Innan, who presided over childbirth as well as healing. Merlin Stone, in *Ancient Mirrors of Womanhood*, describes her sacred spirit as dwelling in the "magic springs of healing":

> Rising in the steamy mist
> In answer to the pleas of the ill,
> Providing the curing waters . . .

Teteu Innan seems related to the Mayan Ix Chel, another childbirth-and-healing goddess who was credited with sending the inundating floodwaters so the earth could be cleansed and reborn.

A wonderful watery healing story is told by Luisah Teish, a Yoruba priestess, about her deity, Iyalode Oshun, the African Venus. Once, when Oshun was bathing in a river, she heard a group of other deities bragging that they were more powerful than she and that her beauty was unnecessary. Determined to prove a point, she took herself off to a vacation spot on a nearby star, where she treated herself to a kind of cosmic spa retreat. But things were not so good down here without her; the rivers dried up, and all medicines stopped working. Eventually the other deities humbly begged her forgiveness, whereupon Oshun returned to moisten and heal the earth. It is interesting to note that in this story, medicine is not effective without water—a reminder of the directive "take with plenty of water" on many of our prescriptions.

When the existence of germs was discovered, suddenly a lot of watery purification rituals made practical sense. The same holds true of water and healing; chemistry eventually proved that some waters contain minerals or other substances with actual curative properties that to the ancients must have seemed like magic. Medically, the heat of thermal springs has been shown to help certain conditions. But now that we are beginning to understand the body/mind/spirit connection, it is possible that simple scientific explanations may be only a fraction of the healing picture. We often need healing that speaks a language our souls understand.

Last summer, my dear friend, editor, and fellow writer Maura Shaw gave me a container of water that she had brought all the way back from Brigid's Well in Liscannor, Ireland, a place with great spiritual resonance for both of us. Brigid is a Celtic goddess who presides over poetry, crafting, and healing. Because I consider her my patron goddess, the water from this particular well was especially significant for me. I have added a drop or two to a gallon of spring water and shared it with a workshop group, knowing that its sacredness permeated every sip. I have occasionally poured a precious handful to anoint places in my body that were in pain. Special waters can ease discomfort of body or mind, simply by virtue of our awareness of their sacredness, their specialness to us.

A few years ago, participants at one of my community's seasonal celebrations were asked to bring small vials of water from sacred places they had visited. We are a well-traveled group; waters from the Nile, the Ganges, Celtic springs and wells, and Native American sites of spirit-power were mixed together in a bowl and then carried in a grand procession down the hill to the nearby lake and poured in. Now, whenever I swim or wade there, I remember these waters and am wonder-struck at their presence in this little lake tucked away in the Hudson Valley. But when you stop to think about it, water from everywhere is continually present in water anywhere. We drink the magical waters of our ancestors. We bathe in sacred springs.

That said, people still make pilgrimages to particular watery shrines for healing. At Lourdes, France, thousands come every year to the grotto where fourteen-year-old Bernadette saw a Mother Mary her own age; the waters of the spring she uncovered there are reputed to cure many afflictions. Hindus, too, journey to honor the healing properties of the Ganges and its interconnected sister-rivers, as this prayer makes clear:

> Waters, you are the ones who bring us the life force.
> Let us share in the most delicious sap you have, as if you were
>   loving mothers.
> Mistresses of all the things that are chosen, rulers of all peoples,
>   the waters are the ones I beg for a cure.
> Waters, yield your cure as an armor for my body, so that I may
>   see the sun for a long time.
> —HINDU PRAYER[3]

Not only the rivers but the rains are compassionate. As Swami Saradananda says, "India, a hot country that eagerly awaits the rain, worships the concept of water falling from the sky. The dark clouds are seen as manifestations of Krishna, and rain is His mercy descending from heaven. Small wonder that the monsoon season is the holiest of the Hindu year."

Shrines to the healing nature of water are still being discovered or invented. From *Deep Play*, here is Diane Ackerman's story of a latter-day shrine in South America:

> In the windswept hills of Patagonia stands a shrine of Coca-Cola bottles. Dedicated to Mary Magdalen, it celebrates a time before cars, when a weary traveler, dying of thirst, found there a discarded Coca-Cola bottle filled with enough water to save her life. Now the path has become a seldom-used road for cars, and drivers stop to say a prayer and leave a bottle of water as an offering.

It makes sense that moving water, especially, is associated with healing; the body itself is filled with streamlike veins, and several Asian healing systems are based on the watery idea of an energy *flow* that, if dammed or blocked, causes dis-ease. Iona Teeguarden, the great Jin Shin Do teacher, discusses this in *The Joy of Feeling: Bodymind Acupressure*.

> For the Taoists, water symbolizes the vital energy of life. We live in an ocean of energy which surrounds and supports us, and this energy flows within us. The patterns of energy flow in the bodymind are like rivers, streams, and canals; the points of energic concentration are like lakes, seas, ponds, wells and springs. For the Taoists, water is also an image of how to live harmoniously and growthfully. . . . If life is like a river, we need to learn to follow the flow of life's river—not to get panicked by rapids, stranded on reefs, or stuck in whirlpools, spinning madly round and round the same thing.

Anyone who does bodywork on others can attest to the fact that when the body is touched in certain ways, suppressed feeling often comes bubbling up. For emotional healing to take place, it is often necessary to reexperience the original pain, to bring it up from the water of the deep self into the light, where the conscious mind can recognize and honor it. Our bodies are often the interpreters of our spiritual wounding, mirroring our deeper truths with symptoms. Understanding the language and ways of water offers balm for the whole self.

There is a popular theory that a vast majority of diseases could be prevented if people simply drank more water and ate more whole, healthful food. I would add that if we could feel loved and loving—particularly more loving and accepting of self—there would be far less disease in our world. Here, too, water is our ally: it has been associated with love since the beginnings of human time, perhaps because our first bodily knowing about love is in the experience of nursing at our mother's breast, drinking in that sweet, watery fluid. Hold the idea of cup sizes—a standard bra measurement—in your mind for a moment, and know that in Tarot cards, a system of rich and mysterious images used in divination for centuries, the suit of Cups corresponds to hearts in our modern playing deck and is linked to feeling, emotion, love, and creativity. Breast, heart, cup, water—all are connected.

Love may also be understood as Spirit. It is deeply uncomfortable for the body to be dehydrated; we need fluid to live. It is only a short leap to understand how we need the moisture of Spirit to live whole, balanced, healed lives. In the biblical Psalm 42, we see how a desert people understood thirst of body and of soul:

As the hart panteth after the water brooks,
so panteth my soul after thee, O God.
My soul thirsteth for God,
For the living God.

The compassionate Virgin Mary, who retains many aspects of the much older Great Goddess, is often associated with water. Mary is often known as Stella Maris, the Star of the Sea, to whom Catholics pray for help, often in preference to either the Father or the Son. Evidently, Mary is such a powerful and longed-for presence that many non-Catholics (including, I was surprised to learn, thousands of Muslims) make pilgrimages to her shrines throughout the world.

Another goddess of compassionate healing, known perhaps to more people on this planet than any other, is the Asian Kuan-Yin (also known as Kwan Yin, Quan Yin, or Kwannon), a female bodhisattva whose name translates "she who hears the weeping world." Her statues and portraits often depict her inhabiting a watery island realm blooming with lotuses, and pouring water from a vase. Stories tell us that she so loved the world that she refused to transcend it after receiving enlightenment, choosing instead to stay in human form until all people are enlightened. Kuan-Yin, like the Virgin Mary, is tremendously popular and is held in great affection. It is believed by many that the act of simply saying her name will keep one from physical or spiritual harm.

The following activities and reflections are meant to open a way for water, allowing it to offer itself as healer, to fill us, take away our pain and our thirst, and teach us how, as Iona Teeguarden says, to live life "more harmoniously and growthfully."

Drinking Sacred Waters

Most of us take water for granted: we turn on a tap and there it is. Do you know where your water comes from? Have you ever visited the source of your water? For many, water has no "soul," no history, no sense of rootedness in place. When we suddenly touch and taste water that *came from somewhere*, it has a special sweetness. I will never forget drinking from my first stream, a tiny one that fed the Loch Raven

Reservoir near my childhood home in Maryland. Before that, water had always come from a faucet, boring and dead. Now here was this living water, surrounded by small green plants, just off the path where I had been thirstily walking on a hot summer day. That stream water was completely delicious: cool, with an earthy mineral tang, alive and exciting. It had soul for me.

The marvelous French writer Colette describes a similar veneration for two childhood springs in her memoir of her mother, *Sido*:

> One of them gushed up out of the earth in a silver convulsion, with a kind of sob, and traced out its own sandy bed. No sooner had it appeared than it was gone again, under the ground. The other spring, nearly invisible, brushed through the grass like a snake, flowing secretly through a field where the narcissus blooming around it were the sole witnesses to its presence. The first spring tasted of oak leaves, the second of iron and of hyacinth stalk. . . . Just to mention them makes me long for their taste to fill my mouth when the end comes, so that I may carry away with me when I go this imaginary mouthful.[4]

Finding water with soul means making a pilgrimage to a place with personal significance or meaning to you. Although this may mean a site in nature, a beloved building will do just as well if it has deep associations for you. I might choose the Lake-of-Many-Waters, for instance, or tap water from the renovated barn I lived in for a short time after the end of a twenty-year relationship, scene of so much inner growth and self-knowledge. Gather some water from this source, making sure it is clean and safe to drink. Then bring it home, and find a time when you will not be disturbed. Pour a cupful of it in a special glass, chalice, or goblet and hold it for a few moments. Remember where it came from and the significance of this place for you. Sniff the water; touch it with your finger. When you drink it, know that you are drinking a bit of your own personal history. You may want to place a drop or two in a gallon of bottled water to drink later, to add to your bathwater, or to use to anoint yourself as needed.

Journey to the Undersea Chamber of the Heart

Most of us carry hurt and shame in our hearts like old wounds. This guided meditation is designed to help the healing process along. You may want to make an audiotape of the meditation so that you can simply close your eyes, relax, and listen to it when you are ready to experience the journey. As with any guided visualization work, it becomes easier and more rich with practice. Be sure to have a journal and pen beside you so you can write down everything you remember after you come back.

First, bring your attention to your breathing, simply noticing what it is doing, without trying to change it. Are your breaths deep or shallow or something in between? Is the rhythm of your breathing quick or slow or something in between? Simply be with your breathing for a space of time, noticing its rhythm, which is so like the rhythm of the sea, or of the flow of blood into and away from the heart.

Now begin to imagine that you are walking along a sandy shore. Your feet are bare; you can feel the firm, damp sand underneath them with every step. You smell the wild, bitter, salty smell of the sea; you hear the hissing roar and retreat of the waves; you notice the patterns of wave and whitecap, the wheeling of bird wings over your head. You face the water now and walk toward it so your feet are submerged, shining like little fishes in the translucent water. The sea feels warm and sweet to your skin. You walk in deeper, water up to your knees now, water up to your thighs; you can feel the gentle tug of the waves. Now the warm water reaches up to your waist; it feels so safe, so soothing that you kick your feet up off the sand and give yourself to the waves, leaning into them as if into the supporting arms of a loving mother. You swim gently out to sea, where the pull and tug of the waves is more gentle, where the water quietly rises and falls.

Now you dive deep, realizing with joy that you can breathe here, that you can swim down and down through this clear water as deeply as you wish. Shafts of sunlight are lighting up the deeps, flashing from the rainbow sides of fish, showing you the undulating plants that open and close beneath you.

Now you see in front of you a large cave-mouth. It may be fringed with seaweed, or shells, or jewels. You are drawn to this cave; you swim toward it and enter its mouth. Now you swim up, up, toward the light until your head breaks the surface of the water and you see the inside of this chamber, this special grotto that you have found.

This is the undersea chamber of your heart. It is warm, moist; you may hear water trickling or splashing; you can hear the muffled sound of waves in the distance. What colors do you notice? What are the cave walls like? Now you can feel smooth stone steps beneath your feet, and you step up and up out of the water, water streaming from your hair and back and fingers as you approach a dais, a raised area with a throne at its center. What does the throne look like? Is it encrusted with shells or jewels? Is it large or small? Curved or straight? What do you notice about it?

Now a figure is beginning to take shape, seated on the throne. This is your heart priestess. What does she look like? What is she wearing? Does she have a mermaid's tail? Notice her face. She greets you with love; she knows what you have been through; she knows how you feel. Her eyes are luminous with compassion. She has something to tell you, or show you. If you could ask your heart a question, what would it be? Take a moment now to find your question. Now ask the priestess.

Pause for a moment to listen. Her answer may come in the form of words or images or sounds or feelings. The priestess reaches now into a pocket or a fold of her gown or a dark, secret place beneath her. She has a gift for you. Hold out your hands and receive it. Look at it. What is it?

Thank the priestess and, knowing that you can come back here any time, turn away now and descend the stone steps into the water. Dive down and through the cave-mouth, swimming toward the shore. The water is shallow now; you stand up and walk toward the beach. The water is up to your chest, now your waist, now your thighs, now your ankles. Now you walk back into this room, back into your body, which you may stretch now. Take a deep breath, wriggle your fingers and toes, and open your eyes.

Reflections on Water as Compassionate Healer

1. Imagine what it feels like to be deeply thirsty: lips so parched they crack and bleed, your throat scratchy, the inside of your mouth so dry your tongue sticks to the roof of it, your whole self yearning, crying out, dying for a cool, sweet drink. Now imagine a cup of water being held out to you. You take the cup and raise it to your lips. Imagine the sensation of fluid filling your mouth, the gratitude that fills your heart, the feeling of ease and comfort and pleasure as the soft, sweet liquid enters and hydrates and heals you. Now take this idea a step further. Imagine longing for connection to Spirit just as desperately as you longed for water. Imagine Spirit filling you with love and healing.

2. Bring your attention down from your head into your heart. Most of us keep our heart-longings at arm's length, fooling ourselves into thinking we don't need anything, we don't long for anything. But we do. Allow yourself to feel what you most deeply desire. Underneath the wanting of *things*, the deeper human longings usually fit into a very narrow stream. What do you truly long for? To love and be loved? To give your gifts and have them be received? Let yourself want what you want; ache for it; thirst for it.

   Now pour yourself a glass of fresh water. Imagine that in some mysterious way, it contains the essence of what you need that will help you create and receive it in your life. If there is a color you associate with your longing, add some to the water (for instance, if you long for more passion and energy in your life, add a few drops of cranberry extract to turn the water a gorgeous red).

Below is a listing of some traditional colors and correspondences that may be helpful to you. Unfortunately, several of these colors are hard to produce naturally, so food coloring is the best way to go. A few drops in a gallon of water shouldn't do any harm. And always trust your own instincts: if a color *feels* right for you, use it!

Red: passion, energy, will, anger, life force

Pink: friendship, love

Orange: positivity, nurturance

Yellow: will, strength, success, happiness, health

Green: abundance, growth, new beginnings

Blue: healing, communication, serenity, protection

Dark blue: psychic abilities, mystery, wisdom

Violet: spirituality, authority, wisdom

Now sip your water slowly and mindfully. Repeat this meditation every day for a week, getting deeper and clearer about the nature of your truest longings every time. Never underestimate the power of your desire. Before you can attain it, you have to know what it is and be courageous enough to feel it.

3. The sound of running water—the archetypal babbling brook or rushing stream—is an old remedy for stress. If you are feeling anxious or tight, find a place where water makes its own song and simply be there, allowing the sound to wash away your stress. One of my mother's favorite sayings is "This, too, shall pass." When we hear the water's passing, it reminds us to let go, secure in the

knowledge that all things eventually flow away. If there is no running water near you, find a recording of nature sounds and listen to it.

4. Tape several pieces of paper together, end to end, to make one very long piece of paper, like a river. This is *your* river. Beginning with what you can remember about your infancy and childhood, think of the major events in watery terms. Draw and write all the rocks, the places of flowing ease, the shoals and sandbars that made up your early history. You may want to use crayons or markers to add color, or find interesting stickers, pictures cut from magazines, or color copies of old photographs to add to your river. Continue with your memories of adolescence. Were there shipwrecks? Whirlpools? What was the river like when you were a teen? Now continue into your adulthood. What are the major features of your river landscape now? How can you identify the most important depths and shallows, the storms and sunny days that have made up your river journey? When you are finished, you may want to put your river up somewhere to remind yourself that your river is perfectly unique but flowing, moving in a way that is familiar to everyone on the face of the earth.

8

The Deep Creative

Imagination, the unconscious, and the creative Source are deeply and mysteriously related—and we often use distinctly watery terms when we discuss them. It seems that water and creativity speak a similar language—a bit oblique, perhaps, but potent and evocative, more easily understood through metaphor, symbol, or story than by linear, logical means. Since the very beginning, people have puzzled over where creative ideas come from; sometimes an image will glimmer up into consciousness like a little fish and then dart away before it can be grasped or fully understood. Dreams, too, seem to wriggle away from us unless we capture them in writing upon waking. Imaginative ideas and dreams both inhabit a watery realm too huge for us to know completely, a realm that is indivisible from the Great Mystery.

Notice the watery nature of our everyday talk about the creative process. Since reading Julia Cameron's *The Artist's Way,* many of us write morning pages daily in order to "flush out" the garbage and "prime the pump." Those of us who make a living with our creativity speak despairingly of our times of feeling "dammed up," "frozen," or "running dry." What is needed for the act of creation, it seems, is a lush moistness, a lubrication of soul and sense.

Clarissa Pinkola Estés describes the creative life as the *Rio Abajo Rio,* the river beneath the river.

> Some say the creative life is in ideas, some say it is in doing.
> It seems in most instances to be a simple being. It is not vir-
> tuosity, although that is very fine in itself. It is in the love
> of something, having so much love for something—whether
> a person, a word, an image, an idea, the land, or humanity—
> that all that can be done with the overflow is to create. It is
> not a matter of wanting to, not a singular act of will; one
> solely must.

Estés's idea of creativity being the overflow of love reminds me of the Tarot, that complex system of images used in divination, and its picture of the Ace of Cups, first of the Cup cards, the suit relating not only to love, the heart, feelings, and emotion but to creativity. In many decks, the card shows a white dove descending into a beautiful chalice that spills over with water. Out of the overflow of love, espe-cially love inspired by or infused with Spirit, we *must* create. As Cameron says, "Creativity is an act of love, an act of connection, a sharing. Creativity requires risk just as loving does."

Creativity is the birthright of every human being. Long before the notion of the special, unique, and often starving-and-tortured artist in his or her garret, everyone created objects of both use and beauty. From time immemorial, terra-cotta pots used to hold olive oil, and woven baskets used to carry cornmeal, had an aesthetic value that went far beyond the merely utilitarian. People evidently loved their materials, loved creating things that would be both practical and delightful. There was deep pleasure in making beautiful things. As Thomas Moore points out in *Care of the Soul,* "If we were to bring cre-ativity down to earth, it would not have to be reserved for exceptional individuals or identified with brilliance. In ordinary life creativity means making something for the soul out of every experience."

In a recent study, a group of four-year-olds was asked, "How many of you are good at art?" Every single child raised a hand. When seven-year-olds were asked the same question, only a very few responded. This is an indictment of something very off balance in our culture. As Charles-Augustin Sainte-Beuve says, "With everyone born human, a poet—an artist—is born, who dies young and who is survived by an adult."

Water can help us remember our own deeply creative natures. The great thirteenth-century poet Rumi, who lived in what is now Afghanistan, wrote in watery terms of the quest for Spirit. This passage, in a translation by Coleman Barks, reminds me of Julia Cameron's exhortation to write those morning pages every day, a wonderful way to begin living life more creatively:

> Work. Keep digging your well.
> Don't think about getting off from work.
> Water is there somewhere.
> Submit to a daily practice.

As one who has submitted to a daily practice for many years now, I can attest to its value. My own daily practice—a combination of dream-play, journaling, and divination techniques—has helped me to feel more connected to my deep self, to the watery Source. It has calmed me in times of stress or grief. It has kept me good, wise company. When I create, I know Spirit; the two are inseparable, after all. When we reconnect with our ability to live our lives creatively, we reconnect with the Great Mystery.

For many ages now, people have understood imagination and inspiration as a kind of visitation from that Mystery. Like the creative act, the gift of prophecy or divination is often associated with water. There have been priestesses whose oracular pronouncements came from the murmuring of a spring, like the one that gushed from a sacred oak at Dodona. The ancient Greeks believed that drinking from certain sacred wells or springs could give the power of prophecy.

In Irish mythology, the source of the River Boyne (sacred to the ancient Celts as the Ganges is to the Hindus) is a sacred well or pool, referred to as Connla's Well or the Well of Segais. In this well, surrounded by nine magical hazel trees, live five salmon that have eaten the magical hazelnuts. Humans who eat the salmon receive—instantly—the gift of wisdom and inspiration. It is interesting to note that in every case, this gift is the result of accident rather than of conscious will. In one story, a boy roasts one of the sacred salmon for his mentor (who knew exactly what the fish could do and surely would have been safer cooking it himself!). Juice from the cooking fish burns the boy's thumb, and he puts it in his mouth to cool it—and immediately knows everything. In just this way, we often receive tremendous gifts of spirit when we play creatively, with no will-driven outcome in mind, simply enjoying the process.

Another magical object that the Celts associated with water and inspiration is the Cauldron of the Dagda. The Dagda is a generous and benevolent father-god, whose cauldron is continually filled with nourishment of all kinds. As Nigel Pennick says in *The Celtic Oracle*, "The Cauldron of the Dagda is symbolic of those things which sustain our lives. Without nourishment, on the physical, imaginative, and spiritual levels, human existence becomes arid and destitute. The soul must be sustained by the essences of wisdom and beauty." Celtic scholar and author Caitlin Matthews describes the cauldron as bestowing "plenty, immortality, and inspiration. . . . The augury or prophecy given by the Cauldron of the Dagda is received by all living beings through the bounteous moisture of the waters that quench thirst, cleanse, and heal." You will notice that once again there are no neat lines of demarcation possible with water; contained in this fluid of inspiration are the essences of healing and purification as well.

Joseph Campbell connects the cauldron to the Holy Grail, the cup Christ used at the Last Supper, goal of the Arthurian knightly quest: "There are a number of sources for the Holy Grail. One is that there is a cauldron of plenty in the mansion of the god of the sea, down in the depths of the unconscious. It is out of the depths of the unconscious that the energies of life come to us. This cauldron is the inexhaustible source, the center, the bubbling spring from which all life proceeds."

There is a hexagram called The Cauldron in I Ching, an ancient Chinese system of divination. This hexagram is concerned with matters of nourishment, or, as explained by Sarah Dening in *The Everyday I Ching* (a wonderful book), "The ancient image for this hexagram is a cauldron, or sacred vessel which held the food for special offerings. What does this mean for you? Your current situation contains all the raw ingredients or potential out of which something valuable can emerge. It is up to you to 'cook' these up into something worthwhile."

Living as we do in an arid culture devoted to the amassing of goods at the expense of spirit, this cauldron image may serve as a potent reminder of our watery longing to be nourished by things of the spirit, to play creatively with our lives in order to cook them into something deeply worthwhile.

The only other I Ching hexagram that refers to a manufactured object besides the cauldron is The Well. Like the cauldron, a well is an object containing water so that it can be used by humans. In translations of the ancient text, the hexagram mostly discusses the proper ways of governing, but more modern versions emphasize "drawing on the waters of life deep within you"[1] and discuss the necessity of keeping our water clear—acting with integrity, and realizing that every person we meet has the same basic needs we do: needs for love, support, and inspiration. Our ancient ancestors worshipped many goddesses and gods as a way of understanding, breaking down into more manageable parts, something too big for human comprehension. So cauldrons and wells give us a way of containing the mysterious, infinite nature of water.

In this fragment of another watery work by Rumi is an inspiring mention of the idea of "well." Here, translated beautifully by Coleman Barks, we are given some poetic instruction on living a life filled with Spirit.

Be a full bucket pulled up
the dark way
of a well, then lifted
out into light.
Stars burn clear
all night.
Do that yourself, and a spring
will rise in the dark with water
your deepest thirst is for.

Carl Jung, that master of archetype and symbol, was fascinated by the I Ching—particularly, it is interesting to note, the hexagrams for both cauldron and well. For Jung, water was a potent presence from earliest childhood. In his *Memories, Dreams, Reflections*, he wrote the following account of himself as a very small boy:

> I could not be dragged away from the water. The waves from the steamer washed up to the shore, the sun glistened on the water, and the sand under the water had been curled into little ridges by the waves. The lake stretched away and away into the distance. This expanse of water was an inconceivable pleasure to me, an incomparable splendor. At that time the idea became fixed in my mind that I must live near a lake; without water, I thought, nobody could live at all.[2]

For Buddhists, too, water is centrally important, speaking a language of beingness that provides creative inspiration of a different kind. In the writings of the thirteenth-century Zen master Dogen, water is the perfect illustration of "thusness," That Which Is.

> Water is neither strong nor weak, neither wet nor dry, neither moving nor still, neither cold nor hot, neither existant nor non-existant, neither deluded nor enlightened. When water solidifies, it is harder than a diamond. Who can crack it? When water melts, it is gentler than milk. Who can destroy it? . . . Water is only the true thusness of water.

Jack Maguire, in his *Waking Up: A Week Inside a Zen Monastery,* explains the relationship between water and Buddhism.

> Buddhism's birthplace in India is riddled with streams and rivers that flood during the monsoon season, so it's small wonder that many Buddhist concepts relate to water. The religion itself is divided into three different schools called *yanas* (literally "ferries") Zen being one sect of the Mahayana ("great ferry") vehicle. Even the basic doctrines pertaining to the impermanence of all things and the oneness of form and emptiness may have evolved from the extraordinarily creative and destructive presence of water in the Ganges River plains and the Bay of Bengal coastlands.

The Heart Sutra, chanted daily at most Zen centers, exhorts the participants, "*Gate, gate, paragate,*" or "Further, further, to the farthest [shore]," drawing on the major symbol of "crossing the water" from everyday consciousness to the "far shore" of enlightenment.

> Winter well.
> A bucketful
> Of starlight.
> —HORIUCHI TOSHIMI[3]

For millennia, water has inspired Taoists and Buddhists alike with its model of the right way to be. Consider this fragment of Ursula LeGuin's version of the *Tao Te Ching,* written by the Chinese philosopher Lao Tzu, a contemporary of Confucius, about twenty-five hundred years ago:

> True goodness
> is like water.
> Water's good for everything.
> Water doesn't compete.
> It goes right to the low loathsome places
> and so finds the way.[4]

Mindfulness is perhaps the key to Buddhism. When we are creatively mindful—or mindfully creative—we draw up sacred fluid from the depths, we drink from sacred springs, we voyage across fertile seas. Here are some water activities to both inspire you and bring you fully into the present moment. May we learn to embody both well and cauldron, fitting containers for the eternal and inexhaustible Source.

Creative Water Play

This activity invites us to embrace "beginner's mind," like that of a very young child, not concerned with "doing it right," not invested in a product or outcome, but just messing around and having some fun with the process.

You will need a large piece of paper that will stand up to water without disintegrating. Watercolor paper is ideal, but a flattened grocery bag will work just fine. You will also need a cheap child's set of cake watercolors—the kind that comes in a plastic box—and a bowl of water. This is a messy activity, so cover your table with newspaper, wear a smock or apron if you like, and be prepared for technicolor hands at the end of it.

Put on some relaxing, playful music. Now, with your fingers, transfer some water from your bowl onto each of your watercolor cakes. You can slop the water around. Neatness doesn't count.

Now, *close your eyes.* No fair peeking; this is all about touch and play and trust. Dip your finger into one of the colors. Does it feel like mud yet? If not, it needs more water. Transfer some more from the bowl, without looking. Did you get any on the cake? Keep trying. When the color feels soft and muddy, mush your finger around on it, and then make some marks with your finger on the paper. How does this feel? What motion does your hand want to make? Your arm? Let your body move the way it wants to move. Try this with as many of the colors as you like, using each finger one at a time—or all your fingers at once! You can even pour the sloppy watery paint from your water-color set onto the paper, if it feels wet enough to do that, and then dabble around in it. The hard part is keeping your eyes closed the whole time, but do try.

When you feel that you have finished, pause for a moment. Try to imagine what your paper will look like. What colors do you think you used? How do you think your arm movements translated onto the paper? Now open your eyes. Do the shapes and colors remind you of anything? Title your picture. It is an odd fact but a true one that often the more we look, the more we see. If you spend some time with your picture, you will probably notice hints of images that are mysteriously significant for you. But if it remains a muddy-looking mess, that's fine too! If you enjoyed the tactile-ness of it, the freedom of no-expecta-tion, then this activity will have served its purpose.

The Nature of Rain

We don't often choose to go outside when it rains. When we are forced to do so, because of the exigencies of our busy adult lives, we usually react with varying degrees of grumpiness, having forgotten the pure joy of playing in the rain. But it's never too late to have a happy childhood. Exploring the fascination of water in its rain-form becomes a lesson in being there, being mindful, being open—and having fun.

So the next time it rains, suit up in whatever will keep you sufficiently warm—we don't want any cases of pneumonia here—and sally forth. Now slow down. Begin to pay attention. How heavy is the rain? Are the drops large or small? Do they bounce when they hit the ground or sidewalk? When you look out in the distance, is the rain like a curtain or a sheet or a mist or something else? What does the rain feel like on your head? On your shoulders? You may want to lift your face and allow the rain to bathe it.

Notice how rainwater behaves once it has fallen to earth. Where does it collect? What reflections can you see in puddles? Can you describe the smell of rain? Of wet earth? What do you see? When you walk, what happens? Do you splash? What do you notice about rain?

You may want to write about your experiences in a journal or make some sketches. What you noticed about the rain may say something meaningful to you, if you take some time to sit with it. Although we may have been taught that activities as frankly simple and physical as this one aren't "spiritual," when we slow down and truly, mindfully inhabit our bodies, we are having spiritual experiences. The body is how we interpret and know the spirit. As Clarissa Pinkola Estés so powerfully expresses it, "It is wrong to think of [the body] as a place we leave in order to soar to the spirit. The body is the launcher of those experiences."

And when we really think about it, what a strange phenomenon rain is! It is how the sky gives water to earth, over and over. We can participate in this weird miracle by showing up for it, being in it, noticing and enjoying it. This could change the way you think about the rain forever.

Reflections on Water as Creative Source and That Which Is

1. I often have my best creative ideas in the bathtub. Something about the warmth and relaxation there seems to loosen the death-grip of my linear, rational mind, allowing me to drift and expand and, well, *play*. Inspiration often comes in the shower, too. Do you remember having any moments of playful creativity associated with water? Try bringing a problem or project that could use a little lively inspiration into the tub or shower stall with you. Just let it be in the back of your mind while you soak or scrub. See what thoughts come to you.

2. Create a daily practice. We are all very busy. The thought of squeezing even one more thing into lives already crammed full can be daunting. But this is meant to bring spaciousness to that crowded life, ease to your soul, a reviving, moist sense of imagination and play to your spirit. Decide that your soul is worth spending some time with.

   Now go deep: what truly feeds your soul? Words, images, sounds, contact with nature? Take time every morning—even if it is only five or ten minutes—to feed your soul. Read a poem (there are websites that post poetry every day) or a prayer, or journal, write down your dreams, look at an art magazine, listen to music that inspires you, take a walk. There is a wisdom to doing this first thing in the morning because it sets us up for the rest of the day. Make this morning time sacred. My family has learned not to pester me when I'm doing my morning work. Yours can, too. I guarantee that you will find great comfort in your morning time. It is one way of taking hands with your spirit, of saying, "I care about my deep soul-needs." Even if it means simply sitting for five minutes in front of a votive candle, or looking at a flower deeply and minutely, it counts.

3. Do some free association with a watery object—say, a lake, or a mudpuddle, or a cup of tea, or a swimming pool. Write down a simple description and any memories associated with it. Then let yourself go a little blurry and loose. What else does it bring up? Time yourself for ten minutes and just write, not worrying about making any sense, even if all you write is, "Pool. Pool. Went there every day when I was a kid. Called the Cabana Club. I don't know what else. It smelled like chlorine. I remember the grape soda I used to drink when I got out of it. My lips were bluish purple. My fingernails were bluish purple. Just like the soda. . . . That's all. Hmmm. Pool . . . I don't know. Pool. Pool . . ." If words are truly not your thing, scribble or draw or paint your ideas around the pool, or whatever object you chose. See where your watery deep self takes you. When I tried this exercise, the image of that neigh-borhood swimming pool eventually yielded a trove of memories, some of which will find their way, I am sure, into my poems and my dreams.

Fire

Introducing Fire

Last night, as I was sleeping,
I dreamt—marvelous error!—
that a fiery sun was giving
light inside my heart.
It was fiery because I felt
warmth as from a hearth,
and sun because it gave light
and brought tears to my eyes.
Last night, as I was sleeping,
I dreamt—marvelous error!—
that it was God I had
here inside my heart.

—ANTONIO MACHADO[1]

People have always danced both joyfully and carefully around the element of fire, that splendid, dangerous, magnificent element whose visible quality—light—is synonymous with spiritual consciousness. Our history with fire goes back a very long way; our ability to call it down—to create it with friction, or flint and tinder—is part of what makes us human. Fire is power—and what a powerful, terrible, wonderful element it is! Moving, dancing, leaping, seemingly alive, flames need food and air, just like us. When it is safely contained, fire illuminates and warms us, keeping darkness and dangerous animals away.

The first hearth-fires must have been such perfect answers to our ancestors' craving for safety; even today, the smoky smell and crackling sounds of fire feel like comfort, like home, so bone-deep are our memories of fire's protection. And fire is associated with cooking, a process that was sheer magic to the first people, changing things into something altogether different, an act of transformation.

To early people, the greatest power of all was the fire in the sky. The sun is the giver of life that brings back the green in spring, ripening the growing things in a summer fruitfulness that climaxes in autumn harvest. We understand this flaming in our own bodies as the vital warmth—the life force, or *ch'i*—whose absence is a sign of death. We also share in the leaping flames of fire when we feel the anger that makes us "see red," or when we know erotic love, the sexual heat and passion that have been compared by mystics the world over to union with the Divine.

Our first encounter with fire's many aspects will be in its fierce guise as the Furious One that both destroys and transforms. We will see the blazing of a funeral pyre, witness rituals to fiery gods and goddesses, watch with awe as the comet of change blazes past us in the fires of sacrifice. We will stand at the very edge of hell to ponder the origins of those deathless flames. Finally, we will come to know fire as the great liberator, setting free—in a burst of glory—what is trapped inside.

After the wild adventure of destructive fire, we will revel in its gentler aspect as light-bearer, basking in the glow of a million candle flames, warming our hands at hearths and holy places throughout the world as we celebrate the fire that is emblem of life and spirit, the bringer of vision, illumination, and faith.

This hot, brilliant element invites our own spirits to catch fire, to light up, to blaze with energy and passion for life. As we gaze on the glory of fire we learn to burn more brightly.

Fire Prayer

Roar through my soul, you conflagration,
burn all my fears to a crisp.
Now send your sparks up, up to our sister stars,
Snake-paths through darkness,
roads for my spirit to follow.
Dance me to death, great fire-one:
radiant is your name.

9

The Destroyer/Liberator

The phoenix, a mythological bird that was periodically reborn from the ashes of its own flaming funeral pyre, rises like a great winged banner over this chapter. Originally an ancient Mesopotamian or Egyptian symbol of the sun, which appears to be consumed every evening but is renewed with the dawn, the phoenix was eventually adopted as an emblem of resurrection. Our ancestors disposed of the dead by cremation in the hope that the powerful, scintillating way of fire would be a glorious road to rebirth.

Cremation is a practical necessity for crowded nations with little land available for burial ground. But the Hindus, for example, who have burned their dead for millennia, also understand the funerary fire as a purification that burns away the sins of the deceased, a sort of final offering for a people to whom regular sacrifices to a fire god are central. Hindus believe that the funeral pyre begins the process of reincarnation, transporting the soul to the sky through the fire and smoke, whence it can return again to the earth as rain, which helps to produce food, which is then eaten and converted to the semen that goes to make a new being. Notice that it is the male generative fluid that is considered central here, not the fertile womb—a reflection perhaps of the status of women in Hindu culture.

In ancient Rome, cremation was a status symbol; the wealthy and powerful vied with one another to see who could construct the most elaborate funerals. It was not uncommon for soldiers to toss the spoils and trophies of battle onto the pyres of their dead commanders, dousing the flames with the blood of sacrificial beasts. Then the remaining bones were washed in wine and housed in expensive vaults, the rental of which was a brisk and lucrative business; trust the ancient Romans—not all that different from us in some ways—to turn a thing of the spirit into commerce.

Early Christians were generally opposed to cremation, in part because the practice smacked of paganism, but also because of the scarcity of wood and the fear that it might interfere with the resurrection of the body promised by the Gospels. The only exception was in times of plague, when it was not unknown for sixty thousand bodies to be burned in one week, as was the case in seventeenth-century Naples. Interestingly, Tibetan Buddhists usually only cremate high lamas, whereas Laotians reserve cremation for those who have died "fortunately"—peacefully, of natural causes, at the end of a prosperous life. The practice is completely forbidden to Orthodox Jews.

Imagine standing before a funeral pyre in Varanasi, one of the largest cremation centers in India. The Ganges flows quietly beside us, and we can see many other pyres nearby. In the distance, a procession is approaching; there is a wooden bier carried on the shoulders of several men, and on it is the white-wrapped corpse of a man, decked with flowers. Family and friends walk alongside, weeping and lamenting. In front of the procession is a young man, perhaps the dead man's son, with a bright torch in his hand, kindled from the dead man's hearth-fire. Finally the procession arrives at the pyre. The bearers set down the bier on top of the simple wooden platform, which they and the other mourners circumambulate several times. Then everyone stands still. Now the young man utters a prayer and touches the torch to the pile of wood stacked underneath the platform. With a great rushing roar, the flames catch, leaping upward, flaring high overhead. We can barely make out the outline of the body through the haze of heat and orange-red flickering fire. The dead man's widow crouches down near the pyre; once, she might have thrown herself into the flames. The heat is intense, reaching toward us in waves permeated with the smell of burning wood, flesh, and incense. Our faces burn. Now the wooden platform falls with a huge crash into the fire beneath, sparks fly in all directions, and the mourners wail. Gradually, gradually the flames begin to subside. Later, when the fire has cooled, the family will retrieve the dead man's ashes and place them with reverence in the sacred Ganges. We have witnessed a great transformation: a body becoming heat and light and intensity of flame, rising up into the sky, taking the first steps back into the cycle of rebirth.

To most indigenous people, fire is vitally important. The Navajo, for example, use fire in practically every ceremony. It is a symbol of annihilation, burning away evil. Many Navajo healing rituals focus on inducing sweating to rid the body of "witch objects and arrows," which fall into the fire and are consumed. But fire will also obliterate things of value, so throwing corn pollen on the fire is considered sacrilege because to destroy the pollen is to destroy hope for the future.[1]

Hawaiians are another group with a special relationship to fire, in the form of the fiery goddess Pele, who lives in the volcanic Mount Kilauea and is loved and carefully propitiated in equal measure. It doesn't do to anger a fire goddess: when roused, she is apt to annihilate anything in her path. Merlin Stone tells us that in 1880, when the volcano erupted, a sixty-three-year-old princess was the only one who remembered the ancient chants that Pele's priestesses had used to appease her before the coming of the Christians, who frowned upon such practices. With great courage, this woman walked alone up to the line of molten lava that was slowly advancing toward the city of Hilo. There she sang and made offerings of silk cloth and brandy, whose fieriness echoes that of the goddess herself. The next day the eruption stopped, leaving Hilo untouched. As recently as 1955, when another eruption threatened to destroy the town of Kapoho, inhabitants offered food and tobacco to the lava, which stopped just short of the village.

Hindus, too, have a fiery goddess: Kali, Black Mother Time, of whom poet Janice Canan writes:

> Oh Kali, vast and voluptuous
> Are your flames—engulfing,
> Devouring, triumphant![2]

Kali is the great destroyer, whose devotees picture her garlanded with skulls, drunk with blood, dancing on the body of her lover, Shiva, with his entrails in her teeth (a graphic picture if ever there was one). Kali is truly terrifying, but her followers say that once we have faced our fear of annihilation, she frees us of it, becoming the all-comforting mother goddess of bliss.

Another Hindu goddess, the loving Sita, is also associated with fire. After her abduction by the evil Ravana, Sita was accused by her husband, Rama, of being "stained" by contact with her abductor. She underwent an ordeal by fire to prove her innocence, in what is perhaps the first Hindu fire sacrifice:

> Then Sita went about the pyre and entered the burning flames, so that all, both young and old, assembled there were overcome with grief, and the noise of uttermost wailing and lamentation arose on every hand.[3]

The great god Brahma, hearing the outcry, eventually said some magic words:

> Then Fire, hearing those happy words, rose up with Sita on

his lap, radiant as the morning sun, with golden jewels and black curling hair, and he gave her back to Rama, saying, "O Rama, here is thy Sita, whom no stain has touched."[4]

Fire sacrifices are still an essential part of Hindu worship. To twentieth-century seer Sri Aurobindo, fire represents the "forceful heat, flaming will, . . . and burning brightness" of the Divine. That divine fire is embodied in Agni, the fire-god, who is honored with frequent ceremonies. Many things may be offered or sacrificed to Agni, including grains, clarified butter, soma (a special drink), and animals, with the idea that generous offerings will be rewarded by the god with specific results. Agni is a hungry god; as he appears to devour or consume the sacrifices, his devotees know that he is well pleased.

Fire sacrifices were known to the ancient Hebrews, too. In Leviticus 9:23–10:2, we see a picture of a fire sacrifice gone horribly wrong:

> Moses and Aaron went into the tent of meeting; and when they came out they blessed the people, and the glory of the Lord appeared to all the people. And fire came forth from before the Lord and consumed the burnt offering and the fat upon the altar; and when all the people saw it, they shouted, and fell upon their faces.
>
> Now Nadab and Abihu, the sons of Aaron, each took his censer, and put fire in it, and laid incense on it, and offered unholy fire before the Lord, such as he had not commanded them. And fire came forth from the presence of the Lord and devoured them, and they died before the Lord.

From the beginning, Jesus was associated with fire. His cousin John said, "I baptize you with water for repentance, but he who is coming after me is mightier than I, whose sandals I am not worthy to carry; he will baptize you with the Holy Spirit and with fire. His winnowing fork is in his hand, and he will clear his threshing floor and gather his wheat into the granary, but the chaff he will burn with unquenchable fire" (Matthew 3:11–12).

That idea of unquenchable fire is familiar to most of us, especially as the Catholic hell, a fiery inferno where sinners are condemned to eternal torment. But how was hell formed? Did God create it? Here is Joseph Campbell's retelling of Dante's story:

> When Satan had been flung out of heaven for his pride and disobedience, he was supposed to have fallen like a flaming comet and, when he struck the earth, to have plowed right through to its center. The prodigious crater that he opened thereupon became the fiery pit of Hell; and the great displaced earth pushed forth at the opposite pole became the Mountain of Purgatory, which is represented by Dante as lifting heavenward exactly at the South Pole.[5]

Certainly Catholics have not been the only believers in hell; as we learned in the Underworld chapter of Earth, Muslims and Jews also imagine fiery pits of torment. Muslims believe that after death, people awaken to their true nature, so those who desire closeness to God will experience an afterlife rich with delights, while sinners and nonbelievers will undergo the agonies of "fire fueled by humans, boiling water, pus, chains, searing winds, and food that chokes."[6] Eventually, though, believers will be reconciled with God, and nonbelievers will continue to suffer eternally.

Some Protestant Christians, too, have placed a great deal of emphasis on eternal damnation—a favorite subject of the preacher Jonathan Edwards, who, writing in 1742, said, "The God that holds you over the Pit of Hell, much as one holds a spider or some loathsome Insect over the Fire, abhors you, and is dreadfully provoked; his Wrath toward you burns like Fire; he looks upon you as Worthy of nothing else but to be cast into the Fire."

Sadly, humans seem to have a penchant for casting one another into the fire. The first holocaust, perpetrated on supposed "witches" during the Inquisition, resulted in millions, mostly women, being burned to death by order of the Church. The second holocaust saw millions of Jews, gypsies, and homosexuals consigned to the gas chambers and the crematoria.

From this fiery and horrific vision of human cruelty, it is a relief to turn to the harmless serenity of Buddhism, which has what could perhaps best be described as a respectful relationship with the destructive nature of fire. The Buddha said that the world will end in fire. In *The Great Dragon's Fleas,* Tim Ward recounts an Indonesian monk's explanation of the First Noble Truth in terms of fire: "The world is on fire with suffering. It burns and blinds. A man on fire thrashes wildly as if he's lost his mind. No one can get close enough to put the fire out, and everything he touches bursts into flames."[7]

Road to Heaven: Encounters with Chinese Hermits talks of a Chinese nun who compares death and the Tantric way of practice—which incorporates sophisticated sacred texts and rituals—to the element of fire: "Very few people practice Tantra anymore. I first studied in Peking with the sixtieth incarnation of Gung-ga Buddha, the head of the Red Sect. It's not the same as the Yellow Sect of the Dalai Lama and the Panchen. The Tantric path is shorter and faster. I was in a hurry to die, so I studied the Tantric path. I'm still waiting to die, just waiting for the fire."[8]

In the dining hall of the Zen Mountain Monastery in Mt. Tremper, New York, offerings of incense and food are routinely given to Fudo, a god carried over from Hinduism, who symbolizes protection from fire. And Japanese Zen Master Dogen wrote, "People in the past lived in the remote mountains and practiced far away in the forests. Not only were they free of nearly all worldly affairs, but they also abandoned all relationships. You should learn the heart of their covering brilliance and obscuring traces. Now is the time for the fire on your head to be wiped out."[9] This last phrase is in direct contrast to the "fire in the head" so adored by the Celts, which we will explore in the next chapter.

The following activity shows us how to turn fire's wild destructiveness into our fierce ally. When we direct its blaze against the things that no longer serve us, we find liberation.

Liberating Fire

This activity may seem deceptively simple, but its effectiveness is unparalleled. There is absolutely nothing more powerful than seeing your unwanted "stuff" going up in flames.

First, you will need a well-ventilated place that is safe for burning, and a nonflammable container. If you don't have a fire-pit, an outdoor barbecue grill works well. If you are apartment-bound, an ashtray placed beneath the fan for your stove will do. Be sure to have water nearby in case things get out of hand.

Now, on a small piece of paper, write down the thing you most passionately want to burn out of your life. This could be anything from a bad habit, like cigarette smoking for example, to a self-destructive obsession, to a quality that you would like to be rid of—insecurity or self-doubt, for instance. Crumple the paper; it can be very satisfying to use both hands in a twisting motion, figuratively wringing its neck. Now light a match and, focusing on your burning desire to be *free* of it, light a corner of the paper. Place the flaming paper in the container, and give your problem over to the fire. As you watch the smoke rising, allow yourself to feel lighter. Enjoy the bright beauty of the flames. Imagine your life feeling different, once this thing is gone from it, once you are free.

When your fire has burned out and the ashes have cooled, you may want to compost them or sprinkle them around a houseplant as fertilizer. When we make a conscious effort to change, the result can make things grow.

At a recent community celebration hosted by my minister friend Kathleen, she invited us to write what we wished to be free of on pieces of scrap lumber, which we placed in the hollows of a large pyramid of fallen branches, kindling, and wood, creating a weird and beautiful sculpture. Darkness fell, the signal was given, and several of us lit torches, sang a powerful chant, and swooped down to light the pyramid, all together. I have never seen such flames in my life; they blazed up fifteen feet into the night sky. For many long moments, no one spoke. We were united in awe, spellbound by the power of this blaze, the beauty of this burning away of all we had outgrown. It was a gift to witness one another's liberation.

Another friend does a similar bonfire ritual on New Year's Eve, inviting participants to burn symbols of old "stuff" in preparation for the New Year. Fire is certainly our ally in clearing the decks of the old to make room for the new.

Illuminating the Face of Fire as Destroyer/Liberator

Here are some fiery ideas to help us in the process of freeing and healing ourselves. Fire is a powerful ally in this important work.

1. A story is told of a woman hemmed about by *things*, trapped in a big, oppressive house that needed far too much cleaning and fixing, constantly frazzled by the demands of her life. One day, the woman came home from buying groceries to find a smoldering ruin; a short in the wiring had burned her house to the ground. At first she was devastated. Her knees went weak, and she just sat down right there and stared at the rubble. She had lost everything except the clothes on her back, the items in her purse, and four bags of groceries. But then the strangest thing happened. After she

got over the initial shock, she began to feel lighter. There was nothing else to lose. She started to feel free. With the insurance money, she was able to buy a smaller house that felt cozy and more right to her. And she vowed that never again would she let herself be taken over by the tyranny of things.

Short of taking a match to your house, how could you begin to simplify your life? Is useless clutter taking up space and depleting your energy? Could you donate things you no longer need or use to a local charity? How can you begin "burning away" the stuff that weighs you down?

> Evidently the only way to find the path is to set fire to my own life.
> —RABINDRANATH TAGORE[10]

2. When a friend decided it was time to burn some old files and other mementos of a difficult time in her life, she came to my place, and we made a huge pyre in my yard—an offering to Fire that roared and leaped much higher than we had anticipated. Fearing for the trees, we ended up making it a water ritual as well, dousing the blazing sparks with a hose as we celebrated so many bad memories going up in flames. What would you like to offer to the fire? If you can't burn the actual things, write them down on a piece of paper and burn it in the Liberating Fire exercise above.

3. If you're feeling low in energy, stuck, or blah, allow the fiery goddess Kali to energize and empower you with the Kali Breath. If there are things in your life that need to be recycled or destroyed to make room for new life, she can often help with that process, too. Here's how to do the Kali Breath:

Stand with your feet shoulder-width apart. Inhale, and as you exhale in a loud "haaaaaaaah," squat down as low as you can while raising both hands, fists as tightly clenched as you can make them. Make a Kali-face while you exhale, brows scowling, tongue protruding as far toward your chin as you can get it. Part of the joy of this exercise is allowing ourselves to be hideous. Stand straight again as you inhale, then repeat the scowling, tongue-out squat-and-exhale at least twice. You will be amazed at how much more alive you will feel after this.

4. If you have pain or tension in any part of your body, it can be curative to imagine gently burning it away. Many healers' hands grow noticeably hot to the touch as they work; heat heals, liberating us from our dis-ease. You can perform this simple meditation as often as you like. Unlike medication, it can't be overused.

Lie down comfortably, close your eyes, and place your hands on the place where your body needs attention. Now visualize the great healing power of the sun pouring down into the crown of your head, pouring down your arms to your hands, pouring out through your hands like sweet warm honey into any place that hurts or needs healing. Gradually, gently, the heat of sun-fire is burning away your pain, loosening the tightness, pouring now like balm into every part of you, filling you with life and warmth and ease. Lie for a few minutes just imagining this sweet easeful heat and light filling you, making you glow and shine. Then, when you're ready, stretch and open your eyes. Repeat any time you need relief.

10

The Flame of Life and Spirit

I am a flame of fire, blazing with passionate love,
I am a spark of light, illuminating the deepest truth.
—EARLY WELSH SONG[1]

Now we have come to a holy place flickering with sacred flame, where fire and spirit, fire and life are intertwined, shining with the same light, the same force and power.

For the very first people, fire descended unexpectedly with the lightning that struck from above, a dazzling visitation from Mystery. While such "wild fire" could be captured and used, it was uncontrollable, subject to the vagaries of goddesses or gods, who decided when and if such fire would appear. The ability to "call down the fire" for ourselves was the most significant turning point in human history, an act so powerful that myths worldwide have equated it with besting the gods, as in the ancient Greek story of the trickster Prometheus stealing fire from Zeus. Civilization, the arts—everything that sets us apart from the nonhuman creatures—stem from this godlike control over the power of fire.

Feelings of fire in the body, though, often seem as uncontrollable as lightning. The fire of erotic passion arises unbidden; it is mystifying,

127

irrational, and intense. In many mystical traditions, this sexual heat is analogous to a yearning for union with the Divine. As Llewellyn Vaughn-Lee says, "Through love we are destroyed and recreated. This is the ancient mystery of the Sufi path. To reach God you have to be turned inside out, burned with the fire of love until nothing remains but ashes." Or consider the following passage from *Married Love*, written in 1918:

> The half-swooning sense of flux which overtakes the spirit in their eternal moment at the apex of rapture sweeps into its flaming tides the whole essence of the man and woman, and as it were, the heat of the contact vaporizes their consciousness so that it fills the whole of cosmic space. For the moment they are identified with the divine thoughts, the waves of eternal force, which to the Mystic often appear in terms of golden light.[2]

The ancient Celts certainly understood the fire in the body. For them, fire was one of two major elements, along with water, in a cosmic relationship strongly reminiscent of the Taoist idea of interpenetrating opposites of dark, receptive, watery yin and active, bright, fiery yang. The Celts saw all of life as coming from the interplay between gestational, nourishing water and fructifying, creative fire. In their pantheon are several goddesses and gods who can help us comprehend and celebrate the essential power of fire; their flames confer upon the seeker a special kind of power and inspiration.

Lugh, for instance, is the solar god of light; his splendor is that of the rising sun on a dry summer's day. Lugh is closely allied with his weapon, a spear that symbolizes fiery vital energy and outwardly projected will; the crackling of heat lightning was said to be his spear in action.[3] Lugh invites us to engage in our lives with creative initiative and enthusiasm. As Celtic scholar and author

Caitlin Matthews says, "Wherever we cast the Spear of Lugh with this vitality, our life path grows correspondingly strong and decisive." You may want to try the exercise suggested at the end of this chapter (*Illuminating the Face of Fire as the Flame of Life and Spirit,* number 2) to experience the fiery power of Lugh's spear in your own life.

My own personal fire-favorite is the generous goddess Brigid with the blazing red hair, so beloved of the people that her archetypal qualities became identified with the seventh-century nun who was canonized St. Brigid (Pagan goddesses may have been out of favor with the church, but popular imagination found a way to keep them alive). St. Brigid's sacred flame was tended for centuries in the abbey she founded in Kildare, Ireland; with a stunning disregard for the constraints of real time, she is said to have been the midwife at the baby Jesus' birth. The more ancient Brigid is the triple goddess of poetry, smithcraft, and healing, all of which relate to fire: the fire in the head, heart, and hands; the fire of the forge; the fire of the hearth. Creative people everywhere nourish and inspire themselves beside her eternal creative flame. Brigid is also the guardian, defending those who place themselves under her shielding; the Irish tradition of making "Brigid's crosses" from stalks of wheat to protect and bless the hearth echoes this old idea.

To the Celts, fire is also understood as the godlike power of thought and as the shamanic flame of ecstatic experience. In *Fire in the Head,* author Tom Cowan celebrates this shamanic fire as the transformative source of enlightenment, illuminating visions of other realities in order to bring healing back to the people.

> The flame of thought in the mind, whether kindled by druid, monk, wizard, god, or the heroes themselves, is analogous to the intense body heat typical of shamans in northern Asia. . . . The explorer Rasmussen found an old Eskimo

shaman who explained: "Every real shaman has to feel an illumination in the body, in the inside of his head or in his brain, something that gleams like fire, that gives him the power to see with closed eyes into the darkness, into the hidden things."[4]

Shamanic initiation is also a fiery phenomenon, as Joan Halifax points out:

> The shaman flies through the Sun Door to the realm of eternally awakened consciousness. . . . The relationship between friction, combustion, fire, heat, and light is the analogue of the initiation process and its outcome. The Vedic term *sram* means "to heat oneself." The shaman is one who has been heated through the process of initiation, and in the burning process has become the pure light.[5]

The Buddhist saint Milarepa also experienced *sram*, but it had its origins in a different kind of fire. Milarepa was once a murderer: when he was young, he retaliated for an uncle's enslavement of his family by killing not only the uncle but his entire household. It was this fire of rage that Milarepa learned to transmute, developing the power to master his impulses by meditating in the high mountains for years. Robert Thurman writes, in *Circling the Sacred Mountain*,

> He turned that rage into the inner fire, which is called *tummo*, meaning furor. It takes the energy of fury and turns it into a kindling-of-inner-ignorance melting into a state of bliss. He kept warm with the internal heating system of the tummo furor-fire, even in these freezing Himalayan mountains where he was living.

The following story told by Annie Dillard about two early Christian desert-hermits gives us another compelling image of spirit-fire:

> Abbot Lot came to Abbot Joseph and said: Father, according as I am able, I keep my little rule, and my little fast, my prayer, meditation and contemplative silence; and according as I am able I strive to cleanse my heart of thoughts: Now what more should I do? The elder rose up in reply and stretched out his hands to heaven, and his fingers became like ten lamps of fire. He said: Why not be totally changed into fire?[6]

The Hebrew Scripture often equates fire with God. Consider the story of Moses and the burning bush:

> The angel of the Lord appeared to him in a flame of fire out of the midst of a bush; and he looked and, lo, the bush was burning, yet it was not consumed (Exodus 3:2).

Later, when Moses ascends Mount Sinai to receive the Commandments, God again appears as fire:

> And Mount Sinai was wrapped in smoke, because the Lord descended upon it in fire; and the smoke of it went up like the smoke of a kiln, and the whole mountain quaked greatly (Exodus 19:18). . . . Now the glory of the Lord was like a devouring fire on the top of the mountain in the sight of the people of Israel (Exodus 24:17).

Catholic priests wear red vestments during Pentecost, originally a feast of ancient Judaism, in honor of the fire that descended on the apostles:

> When the day of Pentecost had come, they were all togeth-
> er in one place. And suddenly a sound came from heaven
> like the rush of a mighty wind, and it filled all the house
> where they were sitting. And there appeared to them
> tongues as of fire, distributed and resting on each one
> of them. And they were all filled with the Holy
> Spirit . . . (Acts 2:1–4).

Many people unconsciously longing for spirit-fire turn to "fire-
water," the alcohol that is often referred to as spirits, and that seems to
offer its devotees the ecstasy and ease we associate with the spiritual
experience. Sadly, overuse ultimately robs us of our life force, of the
very spirit we seek to contact and celebrate when we drink. Here, in
Sharon Olds's "The Guild," is a powerful expression of this difficult
truth. She describes her grandfather sitting

> in the darkened room in front of the fire,
> the liquor like fire in his hand, his eye
> glittering meaninglessly in the light
> from the flames, his glass eye baleful and stony.[7]

But there is also a gentler fire. Holy figures from many different
religions are associated not only with intense heat and fire but with
emanations of light. After Buddha attained enlightenment under the
sacred fig tree, he radiated light. Muhammad is said to have transferred
his spiritual light to his daughter Fatima before his death. There are
countless representations of Christ and the saints with haloes of light
surrounding their heads, which were once thought to be the seats of
the soul.

Enlightenment is the hallmark of the fully realized spirit and the
goal of many spiritual paths, including the esoteric Tibetan Vajrayana,
the accelerated path mentioned by the Chinese nun in the previous

chapter, capable of inducing enlightenment in a single lifetime. Vajrayana uses the subtle energies of the body to transform the mind. Followers believe that only the subtle innermost mind of clear light is eternal and that it manifests in a very high state of consciousness, riding on the "clear light of bliss."[8]

A similar view of eternal light is reflected in twelfth-century Islamic philosophy:

> Al-Suhrawardi, the first master of the new wisdom, called it the "Wisdom of Illumination." He concentrated on the concepts of being and non-being, which he called light and darkness, and explained the gradation of beings as according to the strength, or perfection, of their light. This gradation forms a single continuum that culminates in pure light, self-luminosity, self-awareness, self-manifestation, or self-knowledge, which is God, the light of lights, the true One.[9]

Like Abbot Lot, we may dream of becoming fire—but, as Ray Bradbury reminds us, "It doesn't have to be a big fire, a small blaze, candlelight perhaps." The lighting of small lamps or candles is an act of devotion that melts away many religious and cultural boundaries. Several Jewish practices revolve around candle lighting, which is central to the Sabbath, for instance, when it ushers in the Sabbath spirit like a Queen. In her glorious book of essays, *Season of the Body*, Brenda Miller tells us:

> On Shabbat, the observant Jew is given an extra soul, a *Neshama Yeterah* that descends from the tree of life. This ancillary soul enables a person to "celebrate with great joy, and even to eat more than he is capable of during the week." The Shabbat candles represent this spirit, and the woman of the house draws the flame toward her eyes three times to absorb the light.[10]

Miller also reminds us that according to the Kabbalah, a candle burns in the womb, "the light of which enables the embryo to see from one end of the world to the other. One of the angels teaches it the Torah, but just before birth the angel touches the embryo on the top lip, so it forgets all it has learnt, hence the cleavage on a person's upper lip."[11]

There is also the Hanukkah story to consider. When the Maccabean Jews regained their Temple, which had been sacked by the forces of Antiochus, only one jar of consecrated oil remained undefiled—enough to burn for one day. Miraculously, it continued to burn for eight days. Hanukkah falls near the Winter Solstice; the custom of lighting of candles on eight consecutive nights echoes the growing light as the winter days slowly begin to lengthen.

The festival of Kwanzaa, too, revolves around the nightly lighting of candles. Created by Professor Maulana Karenga in 1966 as a way to restore a sense of African heritage and community to African Americans, Kwanzaa is patterned after African harvest festivals and is celebrated from December 26 to January 1. Each day is dedicated to one of seven principles: unity, self-determination, collective work, family-centeredness, purpose, creativity, and confidence.

Both the Pagan Yuletide celebration of the Winter Solstice and many of the traditions of Christmas, rooted in Paganism, are light-centered. From the burning of a Yule log to strings of lights on trees and candles in windows, people find ways to spread a little light at the darkest time of year.

There is certainly nothing more dramatic or comforting than the sight of a small, safe flame shining in darkness. In holy places everywhere, the flames of faith flicker with passionate devotion. Candles and butter lamps lit by Tibetan Buddhists "offer the illumination that burns away the darkness of ignorance."[12] Catholics and many other Christians light candles in churches and cathedrals to go along with their prayers and petitions. Hindu household shrines in India usually include candles or lamps in front of images of ancestors, gods, and goddesses. Interestingly, the hearth-fire itself is often considered sacred in India. Long ago, it was sacred for all people.

Hearth-fire goddesses are found in many traditions. The ancient Greek Hestia is perhaps best known, but there is also the Lithuanian Gabija, described by Anne Scott in *Serving Fire*:

> The late Marija Gimbutas, professor of European archaeology, explained to me that Gabija comes from the Lithuanian word *gaubti*, which means to cover or protect. She said that just as the fire protects the household, it is the duty of the mother or grandmother to protect the fire. The fire is carefully tended so that it will not go out during the night. Prayers are offered to Gabija, both in the mornings and in the evenings.[13]

For centuries, Irish mothers and grandmothers have "smoored" the hearth-fire at night in a very similar fashion, with prayers to Brigid or the Blessed Mother for protection.

The following activities give us a fiery way of protecting ourselves, and they inspire us to create a sacred place for fire in our own homes.

Flame Song and Visualization

This song and visualization come from interfaith minister and writer Elizabeth Cunningham. Use them any time you feel threatened or vulnerable. You can make up a tune for these words, or simply chant them, repeating several times.

Flame of truth
Flame of love
Within, without
Below, above

As you sing or chant the words, imagine that there is a vital, beautiful flame burning in your heart and that, at the same time, you are standing inside a fierce flame that guards and does not burn you. This is *your* flame, your fire of spirit and integrity and strength. If someone is trying to slander or restrict you, know that you are protected by this fire. Only the following can happen as a result of such an attempt:

The truth will be revealed by the flame.
All harm or negativity will be burned away.
The one who seeks to hurt you will shrink away
    from the flame and leave you alone.

Fire is a fine ally in times of trouble, giving us the sense of strength and inner power we need when facing adversity.

Guided Journey to the Spirit of Fire

This guided journey takes us to the bright and vivid spirit of fire, giving us the gift of revivifying contact with its essential power and warmth. If you like, have a friend read this meditation to you, or make an audiotape of your own voice so that you can close your eyes and relax. You may want to have a journal and pen ready to write down your experiences when you come back.

First, check the temperature of your body. Start with your feet: are they feeling warm or cool or something in between? Bring your consciousness to your calves, your thighs: where is it warmest? Imagine the inside of the trunk of your body, all the organs packed together so beautifully, the processes going on every moment that produce such lovely heat. Where do you feel that heat most strongly? In your belly? Your solar plexus? Your heart? Now bring your awareness to your head. Does it feel cool or warm? What colors do you imagine behind your closed eyes?

Imagine now that you are walking on a spacious plain in late afternoon. The veldt radiates with heat; the air shimmers in front of you. In the far distance you can see mountains. Closer by are gnarled trees in strange, beautiful shapes, and lions are dozing quietly underneath them, their sleek flanks rising and falling with every breath. The grasses all around you are golden; they shimmer in the blazing sunlight. The sun makes a bright halo on the top of your head. You feel deeply and wonderfully alive.

As you walk through this vibrant, hot landscape you become aware of a sound, an insistent drumbeat in the distance, a heartbeat rhythm that makes you want to move, to dance. The sun is setting now, and the sky is growing dark. Now your nose catches a whiff of smoke, that rich, delicious scent, and you can hear the crackling of flames. You walk toward the source of these sounds. In front of you is a huge bonfire, the flames twisting high overhead. Around it, people are leaping, drumming, dancing. The fire is compelling, so alive, red-orange flickering flames with their blue hearts singing a song to you, a song of power, a song of life. This is your spirit-fire, the fire of your life force. See how others are drawn to your light. You enter into the dance, raising your arms, throwing back your head, joyful sounds coming from your throat like sparks. Gradually you become aware that a figure is moving in the center of the fire, not burned, not consumed, but dancing. This is the shaman of your fire. Look carefully through the dazzling light to see what shape it takes. The figure looks at you now, meeting your eyes with vital aliveness. The shaman has something to tell you about your fire: how to keep it burning brightly. These words of guidance are for you alone. Take a moment now to hear what the shaman has to say to you.

Now the shaman points at the embers of the fire; a picture is forming there, a scene that has significance for you. What do you see in the fire?

Thank the shaman for its wisdom. Now turn away from the fire, knowing that you can come back here any time to be revived and renewed. But for now, walk back through the veldt as the stars are coming out overhead, back to this room, back to your body, which you stretch, wiggling your fingers and toes. Open your eyes.

Write down anything you experienced so that you will remember it. If you received any wise advice from the shaman, how can you incorporate it into your life?

Sacred Fire Shrine

Creating a special place in our homes to honor Mystery, especially in conjunction with the power of fire, is such a valuable thing to do. Whenever we spend time there, we find the inner peace and that deep sense of connection to spirit that all of us crave, no matter what our background.

First, give some thought to your personal concept of the Great Mystery. What face does it wear? Which images speak most strongly to your spirit? Do you follow Buddha, Jesus, Kuan-Yin, Brigid? If you come from a spiritual tradition that prohibits representations of sacred figures, perhaps an object in nature will call up your spirit-fire. When you have an image or object that resonates for you, find a safe and pro-tected place with a surface that will work for your shrine; a shelf, nightstand, or tabletop will do. Clear it off. You may want to use an herbal tea-wash to dust it, making it fresh and prepared, and then cov-ering it with a special cloth. Arrange your image or object in a pleasing way, adding whatever other props you want. A vase of flowers or an incense burner are popular choices. But the most vital thing to include is the candle placed in front of your sacred image. Tea-lights housed in little aluminum cups are perfect, but any safe candle will do.

Now, wait until dark. Turn off all the lights in this room, and stand or sit in front of your shrine. Take some time to feel the darkness. Bring yourself fully into this place by simply noticing the sounds

around you. You may hear clocks ticking or noises of the house settling, traffic going by outside, the sound of your own breathing. Now
light a match and touch it to the candle. Observe the image on your
shrine; the flickering flame may make it seem alive. Spend a few
moments drinking in this beauty of flame and spirit. Make a conscious
link in your mind to the figure or object glowing in this candlelight.
You may ask to be in alignment or in service to the Mystery it represents. Feel your own devotion as a flamelike burning in your heart.

Illuminating the Face of Fire as the Flame of Life and Spirit

These little spark-ideas may kindle the tinder of our imaginations,
inviting us to play with fire, bringing a little more warmth to our bodies, our spirits, and our lives.

1. Try this exercise with a partner, taking turns. Have your partner
   turn his or her back on you, and both of you close your eyes. Now
   begin slowly reaching out with both hands toward your partner,
   staying as alert to subtle temperature shifts as you can. Can you
   feel the warmth of your partner's life force? Move very slowly until
   you can sense your partner's energy, and when you can feel it,
   open your eyes. You may need to actually touch your partner
   before you sense it. Now change places and let your partner try the
   same exercise. With practice, you may be able to sense each
   other's life-fire from greater and greater distances away.

2. Take a few moments to consider the projects or ideas, relationships
   or situations in your life that could use a little fire. Where does
   your life ask for more of your essential vitality? In your journal,
   write down the areas that need kindling, the places that call for
   the fiery will-force of the spear of Lugh. Now try this simple yet
   effective exercise. Stand up, and close your eyes. Keeping the ideas
   that need your fire in your mind, begin to imagine holding a spear

in your dominant hand. The shaft is smooth, polished, sun-warmed. The stone tip is beautifully shaped, incisive. Now imagine that this spear brings things to life, just as the sun brings the earth back to vitality, joy, and health in the spring. Imagine throwing your will-spear toward the things that need your fire. Mime this throwing motion. Now imagine the fiery yang power of directing your will in such a focused and powerful way. What specific action can you take now to get things moving?

3. What memories do you have of fire? Did you love to play with matches? Do you remember the miracle of passing a finger quickly through a candle flame and not being burned? How old were you when your parents first allowed you to make a fire unsupervised? Did it give you a feeling of power? As a young girl I was addicted to building small campfires in the middle of my jungle gym, which I would take great pleasure in dancing around. I am still dancing around fires, but now they're large ones and I no longer dance alone. Fire, especially at night, makes my spirit soar. What do you remember? How does fire make you feel?

4. Spend a little time with your memories of fire as you have experienced it in your own body. Have you ever felt rage? Have you been so consumed by erotic heat that your very bones seemed to melt? How can you describe these experiences in words? You may want to choose some hot-colored markers or crayons and scribble out your feelings on paper.

5. What are your direct experiences of devotional or holy flame? You may remember the thrill of lighting the menorah at Hanukkah, or you may have traveled to a holy shrine and basked in the glow of candles burning there. Sometimes our longing for flame goes very deep. A few years ago, when my life was in heart-wrenching turmoil, I suddenly had a deep soul-desire to light a candle in a Catholic church—something I hadn't done for years. The first

church I came to was equipped with rows of little candle-shaped electric lights that were flicked on with a switch. These may have been less of a fire hazard than the real thing, but the experience just felt what I can only describe as sterile; my heart sank when I heard the little click. When I finally found a church with real candles, something in my spirit opened like a rose. The act of touching the candle with the flaming stick, the smell of hot wax, and the sight of the dancing flame were just what I had been craving. When I told a dear friend about my candle-lighting experience, she said, "Actually, for Mother's Day, my mother wants me to show her how to light a candle in church. She says she never really learned how to do it. So that's what we're going to do." What are your memories and longings around devotional flame?

6. Journal on the following meditation question: If I were a fully realized human being, radiating light and fire, how would my life be different? Be as general or as specific as you like. For instance, when one friend tried this exercise, she wrote, "I would take more time to play with my children. I would set beautiful boundaries. I would yell 'no!' to meaningless busywork. I would have more belly laughs. I would invite more passion into my life." Now imagine doing or being these things right now. Why wait?

7. If your fire is feeling low, try wearing hot colors. Sometimes a simple visual cue can be helpful in energizing us, getting us more fired up; and colors certainly are known to have a strong effect on us. Shades of vivid red, orange, gold, and yellow are all known to be stimulating, warming, even antidepressive. Eating spicy foods is another way to liven yourself up: try curry pastes, jerk sauces, Cajun rubs, or plain old cayenne in your food. For more fiery food ideas, see the Summer section of my book *Witch in the Kitchen*.

8. Who are the lights on your path? Which spiritual leaders, holy people, writers, or other creative artists do you look to for comfort, guidance, and inspiration? You may want to get a black paper notepad and a gold gel pen to make a Light Notebook. In it, you could write quotations from your spirit lights so that when life gets murky or worrisome, you will have some illumination to see by. Or you could write your own prayers and thoughts to remind yourself of those times when you have been filled with fire.

Air

Introducing Air

No matter how heavy the earth,
the air can always bear the song of birds.
—DEENA METZGER

Now, at the final stage of our elemental pilgrimage, we are poised on the edge of a clifftop high above the earth, surrounded by nothing but air. The view is sweeping, panoramic; we can see with crystal clarity. This high up, there are few birds, but when we look down, they swoop and flutter beneath us. We are aware of a vast quiet here: there is no traffic noise, no human noise at all, only the hollow rushing of the wind. We pay attention to our breathing, different at this height, and our minds take on a joyful swiftness, darting and soaring from thought to thought. We can feel the hovering of huge wings just beyond the edges of our sight; we grow suddenly aware of the infinite possibility of space. Our consciousness expands. We are in the realm of Air.

Air is so necessary to our existence that most of us can't even hold our breath for more than thirty seconds or so without discomfort. If we are deprived of air for more than several minutes, we die. Life is a dance we do with air, an in-and-out balanced rhythm of inhalation and exhalation. Our first ancestors revered air as the life-sustainer; the absence of breath clearly meant the cessation of life. For early people, sky burials were one of the four elemental ways to deal with those who had ceased breathing; both North American indigenous tribes and Polynesians sometimes built special scaffolds for the dead, which were allowed to quietly decompose overhead. Australian Aboriginals placed bodies in trees to decay, and Indian Parsees place their dead on "towers of silence" so the flesh can be eaten by birds of prey, those messengers to and from the mysterious sky.

The vastness of sky was perhaps the first way in which early people understood this invisible element. It is the spacious wing-road, rich with omens and signs; home of the sun, moon, and stars; dwelling-place of the Divine. Air could be seen in the patterns of smoke rising up to this place of the unknowable, so the smoke of incense was one of the earliest forms of offering to the Great Mystery.

Wind, too, was air made visible—not just one generic wind, but the wildly unique winds coming from the different directions, each with its own distinct character. While air is usually benign, those winds could occasionally wreak serious havoc: gales and sudden tornadoes must have seemed like visitations from some furious goddess or god. But wind was also an ally, essential for foretelling weather, so vital for both sailing and the growing of crops.

Humans have found many ways to domesticate air, bending it to our uses, but it remains essentially an infinite element, unlike the knowable earth, water, and fire. If we include space in air's realm and not just the atmosphere we breathe, it is too huge for us to comprehend. Air has a kinship with water, since, like that element, it is difficult to categorize; each aspect seems to interpenetrate and infuse the other. And yet it is only by making some divisions that we can stretch our understanding wide enough to take in all its vastness.

First, then, we will open our minds to air as the great winged inspirer, a road to and from Mystery that we can learn to travel, sending out our prayers and thoughts, and in return receiving insight from something greater than our finite selves. We will lift up our faces to see sky goddesses and gods arching over us with infinite solicitude, witness visitations from birds of prophecy and angels, and rise up with the shaman's smoke, riding on windhorses to the place beyond sky.

Next we will name air the bridge between our physical bodies and our consciousness, breathing it with mindful attention in order to clarify and change that consciousness. We will celebrate air's kinship with the keen powers of the mind, also invisible but often capable of healing the body and changing reality through the divine ability to visualize and imagine.

Finally, we will embrace this elusive element as the glory of sound—the holy music, prayers, and songs that have been weaving their webs of joyful noise from the very beginning in praise of Mystery. And we will recognize the making of those sounds as an ecstatic path to oneness with the Mystery they praise.

Air is a magnificent element. When we open to its vastness, we are given the wings we have always longed for. Take a deep breath; the journey is just beginning.

Air Prayer

Air, sometimes I forget to look up, and the view is so small:
cracked sidewalk, feet plodding.
Then you push a button; an umbrella inside me
bursts open, is blown inside out.
Leaves scurry up and down your clear highways
and thoughts with black feathers rise cawing, a stream of thick smoke.
Today I opened my mouth, and out flew your song. There were wings
on every syllable.
Air, your hands stretch me open and squeeze me shut:
I'm your accordion, you play me with every breath.
Air of unbearable spaciousness,
open me wider still.
I would be your apprentice, learn to ride on those rafts of
wind, send my thoughts spiraling up to your place beyond
words where every breath is a blessing, every breath is a
song.

11

The Inspirer

Some words, even though we may have forgotten their etymology, still hold a resonance, an overtone that reminds us of something important that we have lost. That's when a dictionary comes in handy, which tells us that to "inspire" comes from the Latin *spiritus, spirit.* Spirit and breath are forever intertwined. The presence of breath in a creature is witness to the presence of spirit, or life; that first breath we take when we are born is significant, likewise the last when we die. When we breathe in, we "inspire." And we "expire" when we breathe out, or stop breathing altogether. What breathes into us when we are inspired? Where do ideas, words, mental images come from? Who is the breather, who the breathed? Every out-breath is a little death, every in-breath a new beginning, a chance of receiving inspiration from the Mystery. It is small wonder that so many spiritual traditions teach the importance of controlling or becoming mindful of the breath: the breath is where it all starts. Breath is closely connected to consciousness, awareness, knowing—a concept that we will breathe in more deeply in the next chapter.

Here, though, we are invited to bend backward a little, lift up our faces, and open our arms wide. We are embracing air as the great sky-road, home of those deities who inspire and inform us.

Practically every culture has a sky goddess or sky god somewhere in its early history, sometimes several. For some people the sky is male; Navajo sand paintings, for instance, often show a Father Sky whose body is formed of the constellations and the Milky Way. The ancient Egyptians saw the sky as the female Nut, often pictured with her entire body—glittering with stars—arching over the earth. The ancient Hindus revered Indra, a sky-god of thunder and rain, while the early Sumerians had their goddess Inanna; we heard about her foray down from her rightful domain in the sky to the underworld in the earth chapter of that name. But whether the sky was female or male, it was to all people both huge and powerful, the light-bearer, the weather-bringer.

Last night I saw all your glittering eyes and wondered
where they were looking.
I hoped for a rainstorm, a thunderhorse
to ride me away from my hideous smallness.
Instead I got your too-many glittering eyes making the blackness
   between them even
darker.
Then the moon rose. All night I watched
as my world changed from one thing to another.

For Buddhists, the image of sky becomes a useful way to understand the workings of the mind, with its shifting and changing thoughts constantly forming and reforming across it like clouds. Many Buddhists aspire to the serenity and spaciousness of a clear sky in their meditation practice, and the "Heaven of No Thought" is the realm of meditation where all mental activity is stopped.

The word "heaven" has sublime connotations in many religions, as the sky-habitation of the Most High. The design of Muslim mosques echoes Islamic cosmography: a dome, representing the sky or heaven, is supported by a square or rectangle, representing earth, which "grounds" it in the sense of bringing the Divine down to human scale.

Heaven is seen as the realm of bliss to which faithful Muslims will go after death.

The Hebrew Scripture makes numerous references to heaven as sky or firmament, a place above, as in Genesis 1:8: "And God made the firmament and separated the waters which were under the firmament from the waters which were above the firmament. And it was so. And God called the firmament Heaven." God is thought to dwell in that higher sky-place: "It is he who sits above the circle of the earth, and its inhabitants are like grasshoppers; who stretches out the heavens like a curtain, and spreads them like a tent to dwell in" (Isaiah 40:22). In the Christian New Testament, too, Jesus is said to have risen up to heaven, implying that it is a sky-place above the earth.

People have always looked up to the sky in wonder. Early people gleaned wisdom from the air; the first oracles or divinatory omens were probably the shapes of clouds and the patterns of tree branches or bird wings against the sky, which some say gave rise to the Ogham runes of the ancient Celts.

Birds have been honored as messengers to and from the Mystery since the beginning. (We have the familiar phrase "A little bird told me" as a holdover of this idea.) The ancient Britons thought that ravens' raucous calls were prophetic, perhaps an outgrowth of a belief in the Anglo-Teutonic god Odin's two oracular ravens, Hugin and Munin, who flew around the world and then returned to his shoulders to whisper in his ears what they had seen.

To the ancient Celts, blackbird, owl, and eagle held many rich associations as three of the Oldest Animals of the Welsh mythological cycle; one of the Gaelic names for blackbird is Druid Dhubh, or Black Druid, hinting at the bird's connection to the magical otherworld. Owl was known as the wisdom-bird not only to the Celts but also to the ancient Greeks and Romans, whose goddess of wisdom, Athena/Minerva, has an owl companion. So does Lakshmi, the Hindu goddess of abundance. And eagle is known as the bird of courage, strength, and clarity to both Celts and modern Americans, whose national totem it is. But then, birds are important totems to many indigenous people, too; the Hopi, for example, include an eagle and an owl in their pantheon of kachinas, supernatural beings that are directly concerned with human affairs. I recently came across a stunning photograph of a Japanese Shinto crane rite showing a priestess wearing beautifully scalloped white wings, in the act of becoming the sacred crane by dancing it. And some of the earliest known human artifacts from the Paleolithic show bird-headed goddess figures with both beaks and breasts.

In our universal longing to fly, people everywhere have envied and honored the birds, likening their flight to the swiftness of thought. Early people learned to use the bird-road of air to communicate via drum language or by means of smoke signals. Today we have radio waves, satellites, cyberspace; the air hums with trillions of bits of information. It is only a short step to go from the vision of bird wings bearing oracular messages to the idea of angels, invisible winged beings who come bearing tidings from the Divine.

We find angels first in the Hebrew Scripture, where, like the much earlier oracular birds, they are messengers from God, but they appear in Christian and Muslim belief systems, as well. In fact, the very same angel, Gabriel, is said to have told Zechariah that his wife was pregnant with John the Baptist, announced to Mary that she was to bear the son of God, and given the first lines of the Qur'an to Muhammad. Today, many people believe in personal angels: invisible, helpful winged guardians who give protection and guidance.

Air gives divine messengers a way to come to us from the higher regions, but smoke has played a role in divination as well. In many places, priestesses and priests inhale smoke as a means of achieving the oracular trance state. Sir James Frazer tells us that in Madura, an island off the north coast of Java, mediums breathe incense smoke to invite the spirits that will speak through them to come in. Similarly, sibyls in the "Hindoo Koosh" (as Frazer calls it) inhale sacred cedar smoke until they faint. When they regain consciousness, they speak in the voice of the god with which they have been inspired.[1]

Smoke also gives people a way to send prayers and praise back to the Divine. North American Indians of both the Great Plains and the Eastern woodlands smoked the calumet, or carved stone peace pipe, to ensure good weather for journeys or crop growing, and in peacemaking ceremonies. The act of smoking it was considered sacred.

Holy smoke is mentioned in the earlier books of the Hebrew Scripture. In Exodus 30:34–36, for instance, the Lord gives Moses a recipe for holy incense: "Take sweet spices, stacte, and onycha, and galbanum, sweet spices with pure frankincense (of each there shall be an equal part), and make an incense blended as by the perfumer, seasoned with salt, pure and holy." The fragrance of incense was thought to be pleasing to the Mystery as well as useful in driving away evil spirits, conducting the souls of the dead to heaven, and carrying human prayers to divine ears. Incense was, in fact, compared to prayer by the early Jews: "Let my prayer be counted as incense before thee, and the lifting up of my hands as an evening sacrifice!" (Psalm 141:2).

The later books of the Hebrew Scripture show the burning of incense gradually falling out of favor, condemned because of its association with paganism. Early Christians, too, frowned on its use for the same reason. Although incense is no longer used by Jewish people today, it did eventually find its way into the Latin and Greek churches; by the fourteenth century it was in common use. Since the end of the nineteenth century, it has also been used in the Anglican communion.

Smoke is also one means for shamans to achieve the journey to the Upper World. In trance, shamans will often ascend with the smoke from their fire up through the smoke-hole of their hut, up and up through the air, and then pop out through the top of the sky. I own a book on dreaming that has in it a wonderful old woodcut showing this phenomenon: a man has poked his head out through a curved starry sky into a strange, layered landscape of clouds and wheels. It is essentially a shamanic picture.[2] But other shamans learn to ride not the smoke but the winds in their journeys. In the Buryat Mongolian shamanic tradition, there are no fewer than two hundred and seventy-five "windhorses," or shamanic wind-spirit helpers: ninety-nine in the south, fifty-five in the west, seventy-seven in the north, and forty-four in the east. These *tenger* have distinct personalities and attributes, like Zada Sagaan Buudal Tenger, for instance: a Western wind-spirit who controls storms in the heavens and sends shamanic initiator spirits down from the sky in the form of *zadai shuluun*, meteorite stones that are used for healing and weather magic.[3]

Wind deities are nearly as numerous as their sky relatives; wind is often seen as the breath of the Divine. Once people began to sail, winds were placated, appeased, invoked, and bargained for. One classic example is found in the literature of ancient Greece: at the very beginning of the Trojan War, the Greek fleet gathered at the port of Aulis, eager to set sail for Troy. Instead, the ships were becalmed. Desperate to get things moving, the general Agamemnon sent a message to his wife demanding that she send their daughter Iphigenia to Aulis, on the pretext that she would be married to one of the Greek hero-warriors there. But when Iphigenia arrived, he ritually sacrificed her instead so that the winds would blow, thereby sowing the seeds of a tragic cycle of murder and revenge.

Most of us need the weather report to tell us where the winds are coming from, but some people know them intimately. Here is a wonderful excerpt from Colette, describing her own relationship with the winds:

> First thing every morning, and while I am still snug in bed,
> I always ask: "Where is the wind coming from?" only to be
> told in reply: "It's a lovely day." . . . So nowadays I have to
> rely on myself for the answer, by watching which way a

cloud is moving, listening for ocean rumbles in the chimney, and letting my skin enjoy the breath of the West wind, a breath as moist and vital and laden with portents as the twofold divergent snortings of some friendly monster. Or it may be that I shrink into myself with hatred before that fine-cold-dry enemy the East wind, and his cousin of the North. That was what my mother used to do, as she covered with paper cornets all the little plant creatures threatened by the russet moon.[4]

We are essentially a lonely little planet spinning around in a place so huge we can have no real concept of it. How comforting it is to think of air as infused with spirit, thick with unseen wings bearing wisdom and good will. The following activities and meditations invite us to expand into a sense of spirit in the air and to be inspired by that spirit in return.

Incense Meditation

For millennia, people have been lighting sticks of incense or throwing branches on fires to produce clouds of sweet smoke, watching their offerings waft up into the vastness of sky, knowing that their prayers went along with them. In this activity, we honor air as the road to Mystery, and we celebrate the fact that the road is a two-way street.

Our incense choices are endless. Here are a few options; choose the one that is easiest or most appropriate for you.

If you have access to an open fire, you can make incense in bulk to burn in it. Dried juniper, cedar, and pine are all used in many Native American traditions to produce a lovely purifying smoke; find some downed branches and dry them. You could also harvest your herb garden to make incense; thyme, sage, rosemary, lavender, and peppermint are good choices.

Small heatproof containers may be filled with sand or dirt and used as censers. Many specialty shops sell small charcoals to burn incense on, and you can purchase special resins (frankincense and myrrh are traditional), pieces of special fragrant woods, spices, or powders to place on them. You can also find powdered incense that can simply be mounded into a pyramid on a heatproof surface and burned without charcoal.

Smudge sticks are a smaller, more convenient way to experience the dried branches mentioned above without the need for open fire. When you burn one of these dried bundles, you will need a shallow dish or bowl, or the abalone shell that is traditional for many Native Americans, underneath it to catch burning ash.

Stick incense is the easiest to use, but be careful to buy a good-quality product, without chemicals, artificial ingredients, or additives. Many brands are available now that produce smaller amounts of pure smoke—a good choice for those with inhalant-triggered allergies.

For this activity it is preferable to be outdoors, so take your incense of choice and a lighter or pack of matches outside to a place where you will not be disturbed. Sit comfortably, and allow your attention to focus gently on your breathing. Are you breathing quickly or slowly, or something in between? Are your breaths deep or shallow or something in between? Just be with your breath, allowing it to flow in and out undisturbed, allowing your mind to grow quiet, allowing your body to relax.

Now bring into your awareness a positive thought of praise or thanksgiving to the Great Mystery. What do you feel grateful for? What aspect of the Divine calls to you today, creating an attitude of wonder and celebration in you?

Hold this thought in your mind as you light your incense. Watch your smoke curling up. Allow the smoke to carry your thought up and away from you, outward to the larger Power of which you are a part. Continue to quiet your mind; continue to watch the patterns of smoke as they rise. What shapes do they make? What do they remind you of?

Allow yourself to be inspired by the scent and sight of this offering you are making. What thoughts come to you?

Breaths of Fresh Air as the Inspirer

1. According to a Northern European folk belief, the kind of wind blowing when a baby takes that vital first breath determines many characteristics of that person's life. Just for fun, can you find out from old newspapers or other records what the wind was like when you were born? My son took his first breath in the moisture-laden aftermath of a summer storm, just as the sun was rising; the wind was more of a gentle, balmy breeze. Interestingly, calm and peacefulness are very important to Reid. What associations can you make between personality and winds?

2. How can we live more inspired lives? Poet Sharon Olds says that setting up the right conditions for inspiration to happen is like leaving little bowls of milk on the windowsill for the fairies—an image I have always found delightful. We can't force inspiration, but we can create the optimal circumstances for it. Some time-honored methods include stilling our mind-chatter with meditation, mindful breathing, or a focused movement practice, and spending more time walking outdoors or simply sitting and observing nature. Other airy activities that aid in the inspiration process include sky watching, looking for shapes in the clouds, observing the flight of birds. Take time every day to read something new; this is a wonderful way to lift us out of our habitual mental ruts, expand our consciousness, and stretch our sense of the possible. If visual images inspire you, visit galleries and museums. The more kinetic types among us might find dance concerts inspiring. Imaginations require feeding, and a lot of what our culture offers us is nothing but toxic, empty calories. Turn off the television. Find a storyteller to listen to. Open to the *idea* of inspiration.

Inspiration came looking for me. But I was listening to the

weather report. I was counting out my vitamins. I was leafing through the Daytimer catalog, wondering if I should order a new appointment book. Inspiration got tired of waiting.
—SY SAFRANKSY[5]

3. Start an inspiration list, and write down any strange idea, creative project, or off-the-wall thought that occurs to you throughout the day, anything that seems to descend upon you from above, any light bulbs that flash on over your head. The more you honor such visitations, the more often they are likely to happen. One friend found beautiful sky-blue paper for her inspiration lists, saying that the color helps her to feel more spacious. After several years, she now has a bookshelf filled with them. "I never lack for creative ideas," she says. "I can always just open up a list at random and there's always something to work on or play with. Most of the time I will have completely forgotten about it, too. I'm always so glad I took the time to write it down."

4. Try divining the sky for an omen the way our ancestors did. Lie on your back and look up. Notice the patterns of branches or clouds. What do you see? What do the shapes remind you of? How can you relate what you see to where you are in your life?

What we see has everything to do with who we are. When a friend tried this exercise, she saw a dragon and a boat in the clouds. "When I realized what I saw, I started laughing," she said ruefully, "because for months now I've been feeling like a fire-breathing dragon all the time at work, angry at everything, constantly on the verge of exploding. The boat reminded me how much I just want to jump on one and sail away. It had been in the back of my mind to start looking for another job, but now I know I need to find one. No point in waiting 'til I blow up at somebody."

5. How could you imagine your guardian angel, should you choose to

believe in one? Would it be female, male, or genderless? What would your angel look like? What clothing would it wear? Describe it to yourself. Would its wings have fluffy white feathers, or would they be translucent like dragonfly wings, or would they be something entirely different? What would your angel's name be? It can be very comforting to imagine a benign spirit who knows you intimately and loves you anyway, who protects you from harm and looks out for you. Your angel doesn't have to be conventional, either. Mine takes frequent vacations to the Islands, where she wears a sarong and sips frozen margaritas on the beach with her halo askew: even guardian angels need a break now and then.

6. Meditate on the shamanic idea of coming out through the top of the sky. When I was six or so, I made a model of the solar system out of a shoebox, with the planets represented by little balls of varying sizes. It took me a long time. When it was finally done and I was proudly contemplating it, I suddenly thought, "But . . . what's on the other side of the cardboard wall?" And I remembered the endless stars over the roof of my house and suddenly felt very, very small. My son recently told me about his own similar moment of epiphany: "The other night, I started thinking about the universe, about how big it is, and I got nauseous." What are your thoughts about infinity, the cosmos, the other side of the cardboard? What are the beliefs that keep you from being overwhelmed by your smallness?

7. If you'd like to feel the power and pleasure of dancing with the wind, learn how to fly a kite. Capricious and unpredictable, winds seem very much alive to those of us who play with them. Find a field without too many trees nearby (trees are notorious kite-magnets), and wait for a breezy day. Get to know the moods, different personalities, and delightful vagaries of the winds.

8. Think of all the birds you know. Which one calls to you most

strongly? Which attracts you? Which one do you notice most often? When a friend was going through a difficult separation from her husband, she noticed vultures constantly circling overhead. They literally would not leave her alone. She decided to work consciously with vulture energy, volunteering to care for them at a local raptor center and finally honoring them as allies that were helping her with the sky burial of everything that was dead in her life. Another friend relates to the small songbirds that nest in the eaves outside her writing room. What do you know about the bird that calls to you? Find out all you can about its habits and qualities. They may have something important to say to you.

12

The Breath-Bridge

I add my breath to your breath
That our days may be long on the earth,
That the days of our people may be long,
That we shall be as one person...
—LAGUNA PUEBLO SONG[1]

While you read this, you are doing something deeply significant—and you are probably completely unaware of it. You are breathing. Easy to forget about it, since it happens without our conscious volition most of the time, but breathing is a powerfully essential act. The simple taking in of air keeps us in our bodies, anchors us to this planet.

So many of us aren't quite fully in our bodies; for us, unsure how committed we are to being here, working with the breath can bring up anxiety. But breathing offers us a road to healing, being a perfect bridge connecting body and spirit, body and consciousness. We can become whole when we breathe with mindful attention.

There are many ways to think about breathing. Science tells us that we have a kind of symbiotic relationship with the trees: we inhale the oxygen they exhale, and they inhale the carbon dioxide we exhale, in a perfect, satisfying cycle. It opens the mind in a compelling way to think of taking in something essential from tree, from earth, when we breathe in, and feeding the trees when we breathe out. How many of us are conscious of this when we breathe? When environmentalists say that the rainforests are the lungs of the world, they do not exaggerate. Many of us are waking up—with horrified dismay—to the fact that our near-sighted species is poisoning the air while at the same time hacking down the old-growth forests with which we are so deeply interconnected. Perhaps when we become more conscious of our breathing, we take a first step toward protecting the quality of the air that is so vital to our lives and well-being. Why bring up ecological concerns in this book on spirituality? According to Thomas Berry, a Catholic monk and environmental activist in his eighties, "We need to regain our sense of the natural world as sacred . . . the physical and the spiritual are two dimensions of the same thing." Breath may be the bridge between ecology and spirituality.

There is a Navajo healing ritual that equates breath with healing. In this ritual, the patient faces the source of power (usually the sun), stretches out both hands palms up, then pulls or draws power in by cupping the hands and sucking or breathing in four times, symbolically drawing the power into the mouth.[2] Imagine being charged with energy from the sun, the great warm light-giver, source of healing. The breath makes it happen.

While breathing in is often seen as absorbing something positive and powerful, breathing out is sometimes carefully circumscribed, since it is believed that the out-breath contains something of the essential spirit of the breather. (This is why we say "Bless you" when someone sneezes; this was originally a verbal charm to prevent the soul from being ejected through the sneeze.) Maori chiefs, for instance, were not allowed to blow on the fire for fear of inadvertently killing with the power of their breath anyone who ate food cooked upon it. Similarly, some Navajo believe that a hunter who inhales the dying breath of a deer will die.

For other people, the dying breath was the key to securing a chief's successor. In Nias, an island off the western coast of Sumatra, the son who managed to inhale or trap in a bag his chieftain father's last breath became chief in turn, since the final breath was supposed to contain the dead man's spirit.

For people everywhere and since the dawn of time, breathing is a magical act connected to Mystery. According to the Hindu Rig Veda, the universe was created by the dismemberment of a male god, Purusha, whose breath became the wind.

In the Hebrew Scripture, it was God's breath—the inspiring *ruach*—which gave life to the first man: "Then the Lord God formed man of dust from the ground, and breathed into his nostrils the breath of life; and the man became a living being" (Genesis 4:7). The Qur'an also says that spirit was breathed into the clay of creation. And centuries after the Bible was written, the great mystic nun-poet Hildegard of Bingen called the soul a "feather on the breath of God." The intertwining of breath and God appears throughout Christian liturgy. This hymn, for example, was composed in 1876 and is still used in the Episcopal church:

> Breathe on me, breath of God,
> Fill me with life anew
> That I may love what Thou dost love,
> And do what Thou wouldst do.
> —EDWIN HATCH

As I read about the relationship to the breath in different global religions, I was struck by the great divide between West and East. Western religions see the powerful breath as primarily belonging to the Divine. But in Eastern traditions, breath can be a way of knowing the Divine in our own bodies, of changing consciousness and even attaining enlightenment.

The ancient Hindu people developed a sophisticated system for attaining the highest consciousness: the *sadhanas*, or practices of raja yoga, which date all the way back to the Neolithic period. Yoga practices teach control of the breath as the vital key to increasing the body's supply of *prana*, or invisible life-energy. Air and prana are sometimes considered to be interchangeable terms, since we get prana from the air we breathe: no air, no prana. Breathing exercises are used to focus the mind and cleanse the body and are a central component in the effective performance of the yoga postures called *asanas*. As respected author and yoga instructor T.K.V. Desikachar says, "The breath is the intelligence of the body."

> Our state of mind is closely linked to the quality of prana within. Because we can influence the flow of prana through the flow of breath, the quality of our breath influences our state of mind and vice versa. . . . Whatever happens in the mind influences the breath; the breath becomes quicker when we are excited and deeper and quieter when we relax. In order to influence our prana we must be able to influence the mind. Our actions often disturb the mind, causing prana to exude from the body. Through daily pranayama practice we reverse this process, as a change in the breathing pattern influences the mind.[3]

Yoga has become hugely popular with Westerners. Perhaps the breath may become a bridge connecting not only body and consciousness but East and West.

Buddhism, too, celebrates the central importance of the breath. Lama Govinda, in his *Foundations of Tibetan Mysticism*, says that breath is "the connecting link between conscious and subconscious, gross-material and fine-material, volitional and non-volitional functions, and therefore the most perfect expression of the nature of all life." Here again, breath is the connector, linking things we conceive of as very different, joining them into a unified whole.

Zen meditation as it is often taught in America uses mindfulness of the breath as an ally in meditation practice. Our minds are so scattered, our bodies so anxious and tense. By counting the breaths, we can witness the activity of the mind and help the whole self become more present, focused, accepting, and still (some methods for trying this yourself will be given later in the chapter). Other methods include simply watching yourself breathe in and out, focusing on the rise and fall of the abdomen, staying concentrated on this by making concise comments to the self, like "rising," "falling." Another method, Vipassana, teaches that simply observing the bodily reactions produced by craving or adversity—like palpitations or altered breathing—purges suffering, so participants spend time witnessing their breathing and physical sensations. As master teacher S. N. Goenka says, "This is not a religion. You observe your breath. How can you say this breath is Muslim or Christian or Jewish?"

Some spiritually connected Asian martial arts also focus on the breath. Aikido, for example, is an outgrowth of ancient Japanese techniques; its very name contains the *ki* (also spelled *ch'i*), or universal life force, that could be compared to the Hindu prana, or the *qi* that gives its name to Qiqung, or Quigong. The great aikido teacher Master Ueshiba Morihei summarized the ultimate goal of aikido as the unification of *ki*, the fundamental creative principle that permeates the universe, and the individual *ki* of each person, which is inseparable from breath-power.

> When one unifies mind and body by virtue of ki and manifests ai-ki (harmony of ki), delicate changes in breath-power occur spontaneously. . . . The change in breath, connected with the ki of the universe, interacts and interpenetrates

with all of life. . . . Having accomplished unification of mind
and body and being in oneness with the universe, the body
moves at will offering no resistance to one's intentions.[4]

There is also a tradition of working with the breath among the Sufis,
an esoteric tradition within Islam dating back to the time of Muhammad.
In *Come and Sit: A Week Inside Meditation Centers*, author Marcia Z.
Nelson talked with Kashfinur, a Chicago-based American Sufi, who
teaches purifying breath meditations based on the four elements. "Breath
is key," she says, "a practice, a substance in itself, a door to, in Pir Vilayat's
words, 'modulating consciousness.'"[5] The air purification meditation
involves inhaling and exhaling through the mouth as a path toward liberation from the bondage of ego, freeing the meditator to soar toward
divine consciousness. Cynthia Trapanese, a guide and representative in
the Sufi Order International, says that breathing practices are a corner-
stone of Sufi daily spiritual practice. She quotes Hazrat Inayat Khan as
saying, "With every breath man touches God. He is linked with God by
the current of the breath. . . . The action of breath in our body is limited;
but in reality this current, this breath, connects the body with the divine
Spirit, connecting God and man in one current."

Attaining oneness of body, mind, and universe can all start with
the breath.

I vow to expand, to take more of you in,
see your shape in my thoughts as they form and reform,
see your step in my dance with the All.
When I breathe, you breathe me.
Great oneness,
I will no longer keep my breathing so small.

Some of us may be new to the idea of conscious breathing, or we
may feel uncomfortable with it. (I must admit that several years ago

when a friend offered to do rebirthing with me and said that it would involve conscious work with the breath, I declined with thanks. Fortunately, things have changed for me since then; the more I learn about the sacredness of breathing, the more I love doing it.) But no matter where you are in the spectrum of feelings about breathing, the following meditations, exercises, and activities offer gentle ways to help strengthen the breath-bridge that is so vital to our wholeness.

Journey to the Breath

Find a quiet place and some private time, and sit comfortably with your eyes closed. You may want to have a friend read this meditation aloud to you, or make an audiotape of your own voice. Be sure to have a journal and pen nearby to record anything you will want to remember.

Allow your body to settle. Feel the weight of your flesh relaxing down around your sit bones. Allow yourself to go a little soft, a little heavy. Now gently bring your consciousness to your chest, filled with the spaciousness of air, a place of lightness. Picture your lungs with their branching shapes so reminiscent of the trees. Imagine the beauty of the veins and capillaries, the vessels and alveoli—all so alive, so busy with their work, your two lung-trees standing so proudly and beautifully on either side of your chest. Enjoy your breathing, the ebb and flow, the comforting rhythm of it. Feel the expansiveness of taking in what you need, the relief and release of letting go. Just be with your rhythm of expansion and contraction in an easy way, witnessing your own particular dance with breath, whether it is deep or shallow or something in between, fast or slow or something in between. This is your breath, unique. This is how you do it.

Imagine that you are inhaling a kind of essential food when you breathe in. Imagine that this food is filled with spirit, connected to everything that breathes, everything that is. You are inhaling the same molecules that Buddha breathed, or Jesus, or Muhammad, or Moses— the same breathed by anyone who has ever lived. You are breathing

Mystery. Now know that when you breathe out, you are sharing something essential from yourself. We leave traces of ourselves behind with every breath, and when we exhale, we give the green things something they need. Breathe with these thoughts in mind for a space of several breaths.

Now begin to see yourself in a place of great airy spaciousness. It could be the flat and windy summit of a mountain, or an expanse of blue sky high above the earth, crossed with smokelike clouds. Imagine the sense of freedom here. Allow yourself to feel the wind on your face; imagine the pleasure of drifting weightless with the clouds. Take time to savor the beauty of your air-place.

Gradually you become aware of a regal figure near you. She may be seated on a throne behind you, or she may be riding on a huge bird beside you, or she may appear in quite a different way. You begin to see her shape, the color and drape of her clothing, the expression on her face. This is your air-priestess, serenely attending to the realm of your breathing. She has something of great importance to tell you, a vital breath of information about something you need to absorb, and something you need to release. What do you need to take in? What do you need to let go? You greet her with curiosity, eager to hear what she has to tell you. Through the air between you comes a sound now, or a picture, or a feeling. Words may be whispered in your ear, or an image may form in your mind, or your body may feel a sensation, or an emotion may begin to come up. Pay attention to these gifts from your air-priestess. Give yourself a few moments so the priestess can share her wisdom.

Now the priestess reaches out to you and touches your hand. When she does, she sends a color pouring into your mind, your body— a color that you particularly need. What color is it? It could be a vital life-force red, or a strong-willed yellow, or a communicative sky blue, or some other color. Let yourself soak in this color with every breath you take, releasing any sludgey feelings that may be held in your body with your out-breath. As you release the sludge the priestess-color in you glows more intensely. Thank the priestess of your breath now, knowing you can come back to visit her any time. But now, imagine that you are slowly and gracefully spiraling down, down from your high place, down from the sky, until you are surrounded by the dear, green earth once more, surrounded by colors and sounds, the sounds that belong to this place where you are. Come fully back into your body now, which you stretch, wiggling your fingers and toes, and open your eyes.

What did you learn? What associations does the color given to you by the air-priestess hold for you? You may want to wear clothes in that color, or bring it into your life in other specific ways. Keep in mind that, in many, many cultures, the rainbow with all its colors is seen as a spirit-bridge, just like the breath.

Breaths of Fresh Air as the Breath-Bridge

1. Do you have any memories of not being able to breathe? I had asthma for a few years as an adult, so I have some first-hand experience of the primal fear that the inability to breathe can bring up. If you have never had an illness that affected your breathing, did you ever get the air knocked out of you by a fall or an accident when you were little? Do you remember the relief of getting your breath back? Opening to the breath is opening to life. Take a deep breath right now, if you can, and enjoy it. Be grateful for it.

2. Breathing-related illnesses are on the rise, especially among children; their lungs are more sensitive and are highly susceptible to pollution. Houses are better insulated, and many common materials around the home emit fumes that can trigger problems; we create polluted mini-greenhouses indoors that are microcosms for the air around our planet as it has been affected by our goings-on. Making an effort to clean up the toxins in our home environment is one way of honoring the breath. Being mindful of our use of

fossil fuels and other pollutants is another.

3. For many years, people have used the breath as a means of becoming more conscious, or of changing their consciousness. Unlike other physical processes that are more difficult to change at will—the heartbeat, for instance—breathing is easy to control and open to a lot of variation. It can be interesting to play a little with your breathing, but be sure to do only what feels comfortable to your body. If you suffer from shortness of breath, for instance, be mindful not to push yourself too hard. Here is some advice from Elizabeth Lesser, cofounder of the Omega Institute, from her book *The New American Spirituality*:

> Let the act of breathing be the connecting link between body and mind, yourself and all of life, nowness and eternity. Breathe in and feel fully, genuinely yourself. Breathe out and expand into formless, boundaryless awareness. With each exhalation you have the chance to dissolve and let go. With each inhalation you begin again, fresh and curious.[6]

Here are some ways to dance creatively with your breath:

This is the simplest: at several points in your day, just become aware of your breathing. (I try to do this when I hear the church bells down the street chiming the hour.) This could be as minimal as simply saying to yourself, "Here I am, breathing. This is the way I breathe. Good to be breathing. Good to have air to breathe." Send gratitude into the air with your out-breath. Draw in the air like nectar.

How long can you hold your breath? Time yourself and see. Try this once a day for several days, and you may find that you are able to hold your breath for longer stretches at a time. Nothing heightens our awareness of the importance of breath like stopping it for a while.

Try counting your breaths, and witness how long you go before you lose count or get distracted. Vary the ways you count. The Zen Buddhist meditation I was taught says to count "one" on the inbreath, "two" on the outbreath, continuing to ten and then starting over, unless thoughts intrude and you lose count, in which case you start over with "one" at that point. Most people don't make it to ten that often. But it isn't "bad" that thoughts come up; that's what they do. Zen meditation simply observes the phenomenon of the endlessly chattering mind.

Consciously vary the tempo and depth of your breath. This can sometimes happen when we don't expect it, as a dear friend of mine recently told me. She had been reading a magazine article on *mudras*: special hand positions from both the Hindu and Buddhist traditions that have different attributes. She remembered: "I tried the whole series, and one of them was supposed to change your breath. I didn't think much about it, but when I did the *mudra*, I started breathing really deeply. It was so strange; I could literally feel myself opening up, and it felt completely involuntary." Try touching your thumb to each of your fingers in turn. Witness any changes in your breathing.

Pause for a count of three after inhaling, again for a count of three after exhaling. Pauses allow a place of rest and spaciousness to form.

Try doing a short panting breath for a few seconds, followed by a series of long, expanded breaths with pauses.

Take note of your reactions, both mental and physical, to these variations on the theme of breathing. Which ones feel most comfortable? Which helped you feel more relaxed or focused? Does any strong emotion come up when you try to control your breathing in this way? Soothe yourself with your own natural, spontaneous respiration.

4. As in the Navajo healing ritual described earlier, we can visualize inhaling sun-power. Pick a sunny day and try this exercise, which comes to us by way of Ralph Blum:

Stand facing the sun, with your face raised to it and your eyes closed. Feel the warmth on your skin; sense the brightness of the light. Now breathe in the sunlight; imagine it filling you, radiating throughout your body with every breath. Imagine a pure bright stream of light like a beam connecting you to the sun. Exhale your own light back to the sun, so that the road flows both ways: the sun's light entering you, your own light going back to the sun. Imagine being one with this positive light energy. Imagine opening your individual will to the greater will that flows through you.

13

The Power of Sound

Like the cry of watchful birds swimming in water,
Like the loud claps of thundering rain-clouds,
Like joyful streams gushing from the mountain,
So have our hymns sounded forth to the Lord.
—THE RIG VEDA[1]

There is a phrase in Indian spiritual traditions—*Nada Brahma*—
that means the Creator/God is sound; but also that Creation/the
cosmos/the world is sound, and that sound is the world. This idea may
bear some similarity to modern physics, which teaches that everything
is energy, even apparently inanimate matter; that everything is moving, vibrating—just like sound, which consists of waves of vibration
moving through air. Perhaps to the ear of Mystery, our very bodies
sing, and the trees sing, and the rocks, and the ocean—even the chairs
we're sitting in. We are part of the song of All.

Sound is what we can do with air, besides breathe. We can form
it into words, into language, into prayer, into song. In this, the last
phase of our elemental journey, we will experience the ecstatic power
of sound as it carries us first to a *kirtan*, where we will sing Hindu god
and goddess names in joyful call and response, then to a Zen

monastery to chant sutras. We will hear the *Adhan*, or Call to Prayer for Muslim worship, resounding from the minaret of a mosque, and pay a visit to the Western Wall of the Second Temple in Jerusalem. We'll "get into the spirit," gospel singing at a Baptist church, and join in an earth-honoring circle dance for universal peace. Throughout this chapter we will imagine many kinds of joyful noise in honor of the Mystery, while we pay homage to the air as the great conveyor of everything we hear.

> In the beginning was the Word, and the Word was with God, and the Word was God (John 1:1).

The idea of magic words is as old as humanity. When we stop to think about it, how magical words must have been to the first people, how divine! With words it was suddenly possible to send a complex picture or concept from your own mind to that of another, via the hospitable air that carried your mouth-sounds. Here was a channel for power, for the transmission not only of information but of wisdom. Words could also frame our devotion to Mystery, celebrating its essence in ways that spoke directly to the heart of the hearers, both human and divine. After all, in many traditions it is thought that Mystery employed the Word to bring about Creation. What better way to honor it than with words?

Remember the magic words of childhood? "Abracadabra," for instance, evoked wizards in pointed hats aiming wands with deadly accuracy. According to scholar Barbara Walker, the word actually comes from a Hebrew phrase, *abreq ad habra*, which means "hurl your thunderbolt even unto death." And magic words were used to open things—like "Open sesame!" in the *Arabian Nights*. In ways that go beyond the strangeness of fiction, words, especially as they are used in poems and prayers, have the power to open hearts, to go deep, to speak directly to the spirit. According to Joseph Brodsky, poetry beats analysis "because it pares down our reality to its linguistic essentials, whose interplay . . . yields epiphany or revelation." Or, as Carolyn Forché says, "Poetry is the voice of the soul."

There are words that serve as a soul-bridge in much the same way as the breath does. Many of us are familiar with the word "mantra," an aid in mediation practice. Brian and Esther Crowley define mantra as "a formula, which, by the power of its sound, creates certain conditions in the world of one's soul." I was given a mantra when I was a young woman by a teacher of TM, or Transcendental Meditation; it has kept me good company for years. But until recently, I didn't know much about the word "mantra" itself. Here is the explanation given in *Jivamukti Yoga: Practices for Liberating Body and Soul*, by Sharon Gannon and David Life:

> The Sanskrit word mantra is composed of two sounds, *man* and *tra*. Man means the mind or the thinking instrument, and tra means to bridge or to cross over. Tra is the root of the English words travel and traverse. A mantra allows you to travel beyond thought.[2]

In most mantra-based meditation practices, the word is repeated silently in the mind, over and over, for a specified length of time; when the mind wanders, the meditator simply remembers to go back to the mantra. This simple, effortless procedure has been shown to slow heartrate and breathing and to change the brain waves, leading to a deeply relaxed but alert state of consciousness. We will have a chance to invent our own mantra later in the chapter.

The repetition of words in unison—in the form of prayer, chant, or song—is a central part of nearly every religion. In ancient times, as musician and author Layne Redmond points out in *When The Drummers Were Women*, prayer was an "active, trance-inducing combination of chanting, music, and dance." Trance leads to transcendence. As Elizabeth Lesser says,

> Poems and music are a sure way to bring us quickly into the Landscape of the Heart, since they speak its native language. The heart speaks in images and metaphors. It makes connections between the visible world and the mysteries beyond the grasp of our mind and senses. Ancient cultures relied on music and dance and the sacred word to stir the soul and create spiritual community. Shamanic traditions deliberately use powerful rhythms and chants to do "soul retrieval" work. The hymns, rituals, and spoken prayers of the modern religious traditions are no different.[3]

When we say a word and elongate the vowel, the word becomes a sung note. With the addition of conscious rhythm, simple elongation of vowels becomes singing. But what happens to us when we sing is anything but simple.

Singing together is a time-honored way for people to entrain. Imagine that you are in a room crowded with people you don't know, different energies ricocheting all over the place, egos colliding, the buzz of meaningless chatter everywhere. Then someone begins to sing a single note, an "om," or an "ah," long and full. One by one, everyone joins in, voices merging, blending. Another note. Another. The sound swells, filling the room. You can feel yourself settling down, becoming calmer, more focused, mysteriously at one with the people all around you, who were strangers just a moment ago but who now feel connected to you by virtue of this common sound. This is a deeply human, magical phenomenon, older than time, and it has brought people together ever since there were people to sing. Singing connected people to each other and to Mystery. It still does.

Singing can also connect us more fully to our own bodies. Hindu tradition teaches that each chakra, or energy center of the body, has a corresponding note and sound, the singing of which will stimulate and cleanse that chakra. Here is a listing, should you want to experiment with making these sounds as you hold awareness of each chakra in your

CHAKRA	LOCATION	GLANDS	SEED SYLLABLE
muladhara	perineum	suprarenal	lam
svadisthana	below the navel	gonads	vam
manipura	solar plexus	pancreas, liver	ram
anahata	heart	thymus	yam
vishudda	throat	thyroid	ham
ajna	between the eyes	pineal	om
sahasrara	crown of head	pituitary	silent om

mind:

Ancient Tibetan practices also identify special sounds that heal and cleanse parts of the body. Many healers today make use of focused sound frequencies to heal illness. Perhaps sound is the cure for many kinds of dis-ease of body, mind, or spirit.

Songs themselves often seem to have mysterious power. The Navajo, for instance, believe that songs are both powerful and tangible:

> A song moving out of the space immediately surrounding an individual—for example, a horseman riding at night or anyone alone and fearful—establishes a zone of protection that gives comfort, for within it is the person who dissipates the evils by the compulsion of sound and words at the same time that he buoys up his own spirit.[4]

Buoying up the spirit is what music does so well; as Sufi master Hazrat Inayat Khan says, "There is nothing better than music as a means for the upliftment of the soul." Even the simple chanting of words on a one-note drone can change consciousness. I found that out when I visited the Zen Mountain Monastery in Mt. Tremper, New York. There, chanting of the sutras, or Buddhist scriptures, is an essential part of the service, which also includes periods of sitting and walking meditation. The simple, and to me often unintelligible, syllables (at different times, we chanted in Japanese and Sanskrit as well as in English), along with the powerful resonance of many voices chanting, affected me deeply. Standing in orderly parallel rows facing each other across the room (but not making eye contact), we chanted the Heart Sutra, which includes the Sanskrit words *prajna paramita,* meaning "highest wisdom":

> Form is no other than emptiness
> Emptiness no other than form
> ....
> Prajna Paramita is the great mantra,
> The vivid mantra, the best mantra
> The unsurpassable mantra
> It completely clears all pain; this is the truth not a lie.[5]

Or consider the quixotic beauty of the Four Great Vows, which we also chanted:

> Sentient beings are numberless; I vow to save them.
> Desires are inexhaustible; I vow to put an end to them.
> The Dharmas are boundless; I vow to master them.
> The Buddha Way is unattainable; I vow to attain it.[6]

Although Muslim prayers are spoken, not chanted, by the congregation, the *Adhan,* or Call to Prayer, is traditionally sung by the muezzin from the minaret at the top of the mosque. The Call is repeated five times a day and at noon on Fridays. Here is author Aisha

Khan's translation of the Arabic words:

I bear witness that there is no God but God.

I bear witness that there is no God but God.

I bear witness that Muhammad is the messenger of God.

I bear witness that Muhammad is the messenger of God.

Come to Prayer. Come to Prayer.

Come to Prosperity. Come to Prosperity.

God is Great. God is Great.

There is no God but God.

The original requirement for a muezzin must have been a powerful voice. It is said that the very first muezzin was Muhammad's Christian Abyssinian slave, Bilal, who called the faithful to prayer from the roof of the simple prayer house in Medina. Today, loudspeakers are in common use throughout the Muslim world. But the *Adhan* is electrifying no matter how it is done, a sound that wakes up the spirits of the hearers, a clarion call that signals the cessation of ordinary activity in order to spend time connecting to and praising God.

In accordance with ancient traditional Jewish law, men have gathered for centuries at the Kotel, or Western Wall—all that remains of the Second Temple of Jerusalem—to pray, read the Torah, sing, lament. But until recently, although women could pray quietly in the women's section, it was forbidden for their voices to be heard there, forbidden for them to read from Torah, forbidden to wear the *tallit,* or prayer shawl. Thanks to a dauntless group called the Women of the Wall, this may be changing. Imagine that you are one of these women, braving violence and abuse to practice your spirituality; stones and chairs have often been hurled at you; you have been pushed, kicked, spat on, and screamed at—by other women as well as by men. But your belief is strong. Together with your daughters and friends, you stand now at dawn beside the wall. As you courageously raise your voices in *hallel,* the sun comes up and the birds begin singing.[7]

The Hindu way of connection to the Mystery often takes the form of *kirtan*, wherein a leader sings a line of song in Sanskrit—usually the names of gods and goddesses—and the group repeats the song back again in a call and response that can go on for hours. I recently went to two *kirtans* in one week, led by two very different men. Both have studied in India and are associates of the great spiritual leader and teacher Ram Dass. Both *kirtan* experiences were deeply satisfying. In one of them, Krishna Das told us that the monkey-faced god Hanuman is the breath of God, the breath of the heart that we use when we sing. In the other, Bhagavan Das exhorted us to "follow the breath," since it is the merging of the self with God through the breath that helps us to gain control over the antics of the monkey-mind.

With these ideas in your mind, imagine sitting on the floor in a room so crowded that a stranger in front of you is practically sitting on your knee, and every time you shift position as your feet fall asleep, you inadvertently bump into two or three other people. There are ceiling fans circling slowly overhead, but the air is still hot and steamy. You can imagine being in India, where it is even warmer and more humid. Then the leader begins to speak. He is Krishna Das, an unassuming, forthright man filled with intelligence and warm humor. He begins a simple chant:

Om Namah Sivaya, Om Namah Sivaya

And we sing it back:

Om Namah Sivaya, Om Namah Sivaya

Slowly, the music swells and begins to quicken. Words change, words are added, words circle back and forth with the tune. Drums beat time. Ancient Indian instruments add drone and tone. The music is a presence in the room, wrapping around us, taking us deeper and deeper. The monkey-mind's chatter dies down. The people all around have their eyes closed; we begin to sway with the sounds. The words change again, the tempo increases. Some people are standing now, dancing. Their faces are serene, filled with a kind of rapture. We clap, we breathe, we sing. It doesn't matter any more if we are touching. We are all linked. The music reaches a peak of intensity; all around are the sounds of joyous connection, a sense of being in some great presence. And then, at last, there is quiet, deep as a pool, seeping into our pores. Hands pressed together, we chant *"Om shanti, shanti, shanti"* and the *kirtan* is over.

A few days after the events of September 11, my earth-honoring community met for its annual autumn equinox circle, a traditional celebration of the balance between day and night, light and dark. The atmosphere was somber; many of us were still stricken, saddened, or numbly in shock. That night, we joined together to do a simple three-part dance and song in the spirit of Sufi teachings, dedicating our sounds and our movements to universal peace. Imagine that you are a part of it.

Crowded together in the low-ceilinged room, we make three concentric circles and begin to learn our different parts. In the center circle, people stand in place and repeat lifting their arms up to the sky and then bending down, hiding their faces as they mime the age-old movements of mourning. They will sing

Grieving and joy, grieving and joy

over and over. The middle circle does a swirling dance, wrapping their arms around themselves for comfort, reaching toward the center, then twirling away again, singing

Embracing light and dark, light and dark

Those in the outer circle hold one another's hands and move in a clockwise direction, chanting

Circle round round round, circle round round

The melodies are simple; all learn their parts easily. Holding the intention of giving our song, our dance to the hope of universal peace, we begin. Drummers around the room keep a steady beat. Immediately, the room is filled with sound, with movement—rising, falling, twirling, swirling, circling. Heard all together, the three songs form harmonies that sound unexpectedly ancient. In a very short time, people begin to let go. Their voices grow stronger, richer. Faces relax, and there are tears on some of them. The three circles move independently, but they are still connected. This goes on for some time. Out of the corner of your eye, as you swirl or circle or rise and fall, you can see all the different motions going on, the patterns of skirts flaring out as they spin, colors, familiar faces. Gradually something shifts. Clasped hands grasp more tightly, energy begins to rise; the dancing and singing become more urgent, faster, louder. The intensity increases, noise swells, tension grows—until it is finally released in a huge burst of sound, a cry, a howl, a long ululation from every throat that builds and builds beyond what anyone thought we could feel, a wild fierce blessing of sound. Then stillness. We kneel on the floor, spreading out our hands, earthing this energy that we have raised in the hope of peace.

Several years ago, my dear friend Maura went to a celebration for a newly adopted baby that took place at a Baptist church. "My husband and I were the only white people there," she remembers. "I guess we could have felt a little different or awkward, but once the singing started, it was the most amazing thing. I had never been with singing like that before. I was so uplifted, I could really feel the spirit, it was so alive. The energy was just phenomenal. And I felt completely at home and welcomed."

Imagine sitting on a crowded church pew as the choir leader begins a simple rhythmic song of gratitude for new life, a song of great joy. Now the rich textures of the chorus come in, amplifying the beat, encouraging us to sing, harmonies weaving and interweaving. The tune and rhythm are infectious: it's impossible to keep still. Feet tap, hands clap, bodies sway. Soon the whole room is rocking with joyful noise. This room of strangers has become family—part of the great, complicated, but so simple human family to which we all belong. Everyone is smiling; every heart is open and filled with thanks.

The meditations and activities that follow are all different ways of experiencing the power of air as word and song. May our encounters with sound bring us a greater sense of aliveness, closeness to others, and connectedness to Mystery, however we conceive of it. May we honor the air for being our willing conduit. May the sounds we make be a blessing to the earth, to the water, to the fire, to the air, for the good of all. May it be so.

Sound Prayer

Prayer does not have to be just the rote repetition of words you have been taught. As poet Elizabeth Cunningham reminds us, "You can only pray what's in your heart." Take a little time now to close your eyes and go deeper. Bring your energy down from your head into your heart-center. Allow yourself to feel whatever it is you are feeling right now. What is in your heart at this moment? Peace? Stress? Grief? Anger? When I go to my heart, I am often aware of sadness, mixed with a hope of hope. What is the truth in your heart?

Open your mouth now, take in a deep breath, and, keeping your heart-truth in mind, allow a sound to come out. It can be any sound— a groan, a giggle, a howl, a long, true note—whatever wants to sing through you, allow the sound to flow. Imagine that the great spirit permeating all is carrying your sound on its wings, accepting it, transforming it. If your sound wants to shift and change, allow this to happen. If feelings come up, let them.

Julia Cameron tells a very moving story in *Vein of Gold* about doing a meditation like this one: "I began to 'sing' my dead mother, whom I miss but seldom weep for. Within minutes, tears were rolling freely down my face. I was contacting and healing a grief that I had carried, frozen, for a decade and a half."

Sound has the magical ability to unlock, to release, to heal. While I was in the painful midst of my relationship breakup, I began playing Beethoven's Ninth Symphony over and over at top volume whenever I was alone. That magnificent music released huge feelings in me—feelings I had to suppress when I was with other people—and I was finally able to weep and wail and rage. It was the most cathartic thing I have ever done; I like to think that Beethoven was my ally in getting through the ordeal. As the poet John Dryden said, "What passion cannot music raise and quell?"

Breaths of Fresh Air as the Power of Sound

1. The Kaluli tribe in Papua New Guinea tell the time of day by the kinds of birdsongs in the tropical rainforest around them. When performing tasks—clearing a garden, for instance—the people sing and chant in rhythm with these sounds. Their lives are completely oriented to, and interwoven with, the sounds of nature.[8]

   When we stop and pay attention, we can notice the sounds that keep us company at different hours of the day, even if we live in the city. Waking-up birdsong, schoolbuses going by, and off-to-work traffic, for instance, all signal early morning. I have fallen in love with the hourly church bells on this village street; they are my reminder to be thankful not only for my breathing but for being alive and on the planet. What are the sounds where you are? How can you interact with or become more grateful for them?

2. What are your favorite words? Which words stimulate or inspire you? The lovely, melodic "anemone" is usually listed as a favorite among English-language speakers. Today, my own list would

include the words "tempest," "smoke," and "pleasure." Tomorrow, I might prefer "hyacinth" or "confirmation." It is good to love words. Think of a few that attract you.

3. The word "language" comes from the Latin word for "tongue." While we are all familiar with the phrase "mother tongue," my friend Gary recently told me a story that perfectly sums up its power.

Gary's heritage is Jewish, but not his spirituality. "In fact," he remembers, "to tell the truth, most of my childhood memories of synagogue were fairly unpleasant ones of sitting still for hours at a time, not really being into it." But when his mother died and it fell on him to arrange the funeral, he wanted to give her the traditional ceremony she would have wanted. "At the funeral I was keeping my composure," he says. "I was numb, really. It wasn't until the rabbi started singing in Hebrew that I was able to cry. I hadn't realized how powerful that language was for me. It was my mother tongue."

What is your mother tongue? What languages did your people speak? For me, the sound of Gaelic is deeply stirring; prayers and songs in Irish or Scots Gaelic have a special beauty. You may want to seek out hymns, prayers, and songs in your ancestral language to learn.

4. You can invent your own personal mantra to become the corner-stone of a meditation practice. First, begin to think about the sounds that your mouth enjoys making. When my son was just learning to speak, plosive and percussive sounds were his favorites: he would turn every "m" into "b," although he was perfectly capable of making the "m" sound (he called me "Baba," not "Mama"). I have always taken this as early proof of his strong will, but since he has developed a passion for drumming, it makes even more sense. What sounds are you drawn to? Choose three consonant sounds that are your favorites (today, mine would be "l," "n," and "r"). Now

choose two or three vowel sounds that are especially beautiful to you (I'm partial to a long "oo" and "ah.") Simply playing with the sounds, put them together to create a two- or three-syllable non-sense word that is pleasing to you. It is better not to write it down: you will keep this word-sound in your mind only.

When you are ready to try this form of meditation, simply sit comfortably with your eyes closed, and repeat your mantra silently to yourself for twenty minutes. If you need to scratch or sneeze or shift position, go right ahead. You can also peek at your clock to check the time. When you start to think about what to make for dinner, or your next dentist appointment, just gently bring your awareness back to your mantra.

5. Honor air in the form of magic words by reading more poetry out loud. Share your favorite poems with friends. You could form a group that meets to read poetry aloud—a most inspiring and enlivening thing to do. You may find you are moved to write some poetry yourselves.

6. What sounds make you feel joyful, alive, closer to Spirit? For some of us, the noise of flowing water, or ocean waves, or birdsong, or wind in the trees makes us feel peaceful and connected. For others, a particular kind of music—Mozart, the driving beat of African drumming, or the ethereal sound of an Andean flute—bring us to a place of deeper and more intense aliveness. Make note of your own spirit-trigger sounds.

7. Do you ever get songs stuck in your head? If you find yourself going round and round with a particular song, stop and listen to the words. It is uncanny how appropriate they often are, how insightful a message they are to you about the state of your body/spirit/mind. To go deeper with this particular idea, ask yourself the question posed by Caitlin Matthews in her *Celtic Wisdom Tarot*: "What song is guiding you at this time?" Do you have a beacon song? In the darkest part of my recent journey, I found com-

fort in a fragment of hymn I remembered from an old record my mother used to play: the Mormon Tabernacle choir singing, "The night is dark and I am far from home, lead Thou me on." A song to the goddess Brigid, composed at a community celebration, was also helpful to me. What songs comfort, inspire, and guide you?

8. What effects do different kinds of music have on you? I have learned to be careful about exposing myself to some of the violent, agitated, angry music that is so popular today. When I hear too much of it, I feel desperately stressed, nerve-wracked, dis-eased. By contrast, most Baroque music seems to possess a magical power to make me feel safe, tranquil, and happy. As Dr. John Diamond says, "Surrounded by the right sounds, we all can be invigorated, energized, and balanced." What frequencies resonate for you?

At a recent Tibetan singing bowl concert, the sounds sent all of us into what I can only describe as an altered state: every single one of us experienced an uplifting sense of profound calm, a cellular-level shift, the effects of which I felt for several days afterward. Take time to hear more music that soothes and uplifts you, and less that assaults and harms you. Invest in earphones for your impervious teens. Expose them to the music that speaks the language of your soul and see how they respond. Surprisingly, my drummer son truly enjoyed his first *kirtan*, singing along heartily and beating out the rhythms with his hands and feet.

9. A prayer and singing circle meets every month at my community center, where we improvise, sing familiar hymns and chants, sing for peace, sing for healing—and have a wonderful time. You may want to start a singing circle in your own community. So many of us are hungry for direct experience of spirit, and singing feeds that hunger so beautifully, overcoming religious, racial, and socioeconomic barriers with ease. Some of my most powerful experiences with the numinous have been when I'm singing. When the chills start running up and down my body and tears come to my eyes, I know I am in the presence of the Mystery. Find a group of friends

and start singing together. Amazing things can happen.

Notes

Introducing Earth

1. From "These Days," by Charles Olson, in *The Collected Poems of Charles Olson*, ed. George F. Butterick (Berkeley: University of California Press, 1987), p. 106.

Chapter 1

1. Marija Gimbutas, *The Language of the Goddess*.
2. Circle song, source unknown.
3. Another circle song, source unknown.
4. Rumi, *The Illuminated Rumi*, trans. by Coleman Barks (New York: Broadway Books, 1997), p. 75.

Chapter 2

1. Merlin Stone, *Ancient Mirrors of Womanhood* (Boston: Beacon Press, 1990), p. 355.
2. Ancient song of Celtic shamanism as taught by Tom Cowan.
3. Ancient shaman-song quoted by Joan Halifax in *Shaman: The Wounded Healer* (London: Thames and Hudson, 1982), p. 59.
4. Rainer Maria Rilke, from "I have many brothers in the South" in *The Soul Is Here for Its Own Joy*, ed. Robert Bly (Hopewell, N.J.: Ecco Press, 1995), p. 36.

Chapter 3

1. Excerpt from an old Irish prayer translated by Caitlin Matthews, *The Celtic Spirit* (San Francisco: HarperSanFrancisco, 1999), p. 157.

2. Rachel Pollack, *Shining Woman Tarot Guide* (London: Aquarian Press, 1992), p. 114.

3. Joseph Campbell, *The Power of Myth* (New York: Doubleday, 1988), pp. 79–80.

4. Lama Kunga Rimpoche and Brian Cutillo, trans., "Stories and Songs from the Oral Tradition of Jetsun Milarepa," in *Drinking the Mountain Stream* (New York: Latsawa, 1978), pp. 56–57.

5. Zen anecdote retold by Manuela Dunn Mascetti in *The Little Book of Zen: Haiku, Koans, Sayings* (New York: Barnes & Noble Books, 2001), p. 137.

6. Carl Jung, *Memories, Dreams, Reflections* (New York: Vintage Books, 1989), pp. 77–78.

7. Kazuaki Tanahashi, ed., *Moon in a Dewdrop: Writings of Zen Master Dogen* (New York: Farrar, Straus and Giroux, 1985), p. 97.

8. Bill Porter, *Road to Heaven: Encounters with Chinese Hermits* (San Francisco: Mercury House, 1993), p. 196.

9. David Rosen, *The Tao of Jung* (New York: Penguin, 1996), pp. 141–146.

CHAPTER 4

1. Barbara Walker, *The Woman's Encyclopedia of Myths and Secrets* (San Francisco: Harper and Row, 1983), p. 768.

2. Elizabeth Roberts and Elias Amidon, eds., *Earth Prayers* (San Francisco: HarperSanFrancisco, 1991), p. 5.

3. Sappho, trans. by Charoula, *Return of the Great Goddess*, ed. Burleigh Muten (Boston: Shambhala, 1994), p. 158.

4. Elizabeth Cunningham, *Small Bird: Poems & Prayers* (Barrytown, N.Y.: Station Hill Press, 2000), p. 75.

5. Rumi, *The Illuminated Rumi*, trans. Barks, p. 34.

6. Tanahashi, ed., *Moon in a Dewdrop*, p. 114.

7. Kenneth Rexroth, "Hojoki," *Big Sky Mind: Buddhism and the Beat Generation* (New York: Riverhead Books, 1995), pp. 326–327.

8. Julian of Norwich, in Roberts and Amidon, eds., *Earth Prayers*, p. 373.

9. Clarissa Pinkola Estés, *Women Who Run with the Wolves* (New York: Ballantine, 1992), p. 100.

10. Kabir, trans. by Robert Bly, in *The Soul Is Here for Its Own Joy*, ed. Robert Bly (Hopewell, N.J.: Ecco Press, 1995), p. 93.

CHAPTER 6

1. Elizabeth Roberts and Elias Amidon, eds., *Honoring the Earth: A Journal of New Earth Prayers* (San Francisco: HarperSanFrancisco, 1997), n.p.
2. Robert A. F. Thurman, *Inside Tibetan Buddhism: Rituals and Symbols Revealed* (San Francisco: Collins Publishers, 1995), pp. 72–76.
3. Burleigh Mutén, ed., *Her Words: An Anthology of Poetry about the Great Goddess* (Boston: Shambhala, 1999), p. 205.

CHAPTER 7

1. Anon. Welsh chronicle, trans. by Caitlin Matthews, *The Celtic Spirit: Daily Meditations for the Turning Year* (San Francisco: HarperSanFrancisco, 1999), p. 158.
2. Thomas Bulfinch, *Bulfinch's Mythology* (New York: Random House, 1993), p. 163.
3. Roberts and Amidon, eds., *Earth Prayers*, p. 153.
4. Colette, in Michele Sarde, *Colette: A Biography,* trans. Richard Miller (New York: William Morrow and Co., 1980), pp. 39–40.

CHAPTER 8

1. Sarah Dening, *The Everyday I Ching* (New York: St. Martin's Press, 1995), pp. 152–153.
2. C. G. Jung, *Memories, Dreams, Reflections,* p. 7.
3. Mascetti, ed., *The Little Book of Zen,* p. 51.
4. Ursula LeGuin, *Lao Tzu: Tao Te Ching: A Book about the Way and the Power of the Way* (Boston: Shambhala, 1997), p. 11.

INTRODUCING FIRE

1. Antonio Machado, "Last Night," translated by Robert Bly, in *The Rag and Bone Shop of the Heart,* ed. Robert Bly, James Hillman, and Michael Meade (New York: HarperCollins, 1992), pp. 372–373.

CHAPTER 9

1. Gladys A. Reichard, *Navaho Religion* (Princeton: Princeton University Press, 1955), pp. 554–555.
2. Janine Canan, "Oh Kali," in *Her Words,* ed. Mutén, p. 175.

3. Sister Nivedita and Ananda K. Coomaraswamy, *Hindus and Buddhists: Myths and Legends* (London: Studio Editions, 1994), pp. 98–99.

4. Ibid.

5. Diane K. Osbon, ed., *Reflections on the Art of Living: A Joseph Campbell Companion* (New York: HarperCollins, 1991), p. 150.

6. Mary Pat Fisher, *Living Religions* (Upper Saddle River, N.J.: Prentice-Hall, 1999), p. 359.

7. Tim Ward, *The Great Dragon's Fleas* (Berkeley: Celestial Arts, 1993), p. 134.

8. Porter, *Road to Heaven*, p. 109.

9. Tanahashi, ed., *Moon in a Dewdrop*, p. 50.

10. Rabindranath Tagore, in *The Soul Is Here for Its Own Joy*, ed. Robert Bly, p. 150.

CHAPTER 10

1. Tom Cowan, *Fire in the Head: Shamanism and the Celtic Spirit* (San Francisco: HarperSanFrancisco, 1993), p. 45.

2. Walker, *The Woman's Encyclopedia of Myths and Secrets*, p. 917.

3. Nigel Pennick, *The Celtic Oracle* (London: The Aquarian Press, 1992), p. 76.

4. Cowan, *Fire in the Head*, p. 39.

5. Joan Halifax, *Shaman: The Wounded Healer* (London: Thames and Hudson, 1982), p. 25.

6. Annie Dillard, *For the Time Being* (New York: Vintage Books, 2000), p. 180.

7. Sharon Olds, "The Guild," in *The Rag and Bone Shop of the Heart*, ed. Bly, Hillman, and Meade, p. 129.

8. Mary Pat Fisher, *Living Religions*, p. 162.

9. Merriam-Webster's *Encyclopedia of World Religions* (Springfield, Mass.: Merriam-Webster, Inc.), p. 531.

10. Brenda Miller, *Season of the Body* (Louisville, Ky.: Sarabande Books, 2002), p. 38.

11. Miller, p. 49.

12. Thurman, *Inside Tibetan Buddhism*, p. 49.

13. Anne Scott, *Serving Fire: Food for Thought, Body, and Soul* (Berkeley: Celestial Arts, 1994), p. 13.

CHAPTER 11

1. Sir James G. Frazer, *The Golden Bough: A Study in Magic and Religion* (New York: Macmillan, 1951), pp. 109–110.

2. This image appears on the back cover of Dick McLeester, *Welcome to the Magic Theatre: A Handbook for Exploring Dreams* (Amherst, Mass.: Food for Thought Publications, 1976).

3. Sarangerel, *Chosen by the Spirits: Following Your Shamanic Calling* (Rochester, Vt.: Inner Traditions, 2001).

4. Colette, *My Mother's House and Sido*, trans. Enid McLeod (New York: Farrar, Straus and Giroux, 1953), pp. 159–160.

5. Sy Syfransky, *Sun* 317 (May 2002): 47.

CHAPTER 12

1. Roberts and Amidon, eds., *Honoring the Earth*, n.p.

2. Reichard, *Navaho Religion*, p. 529.

3. T.K.V. Desikachar, *The Heart of Yoga: Developing a Personal Practice* (Rochester, Vt.: Inner Traditions, 1995), pp. 54–55.

4. Kisshomaru Ueshiba, *The Spirit of Aikido* (New York: Harper and Row, 1987), pp. 15, 24.

5. Marcia Z. Nelson, *Come and Sit: A Week Inside Meditation Centers* (Woodstock, Vt.: SkyLight Paths, 2001), pp. 152–153.

6. Elizabeth Lesser, *The New American Spirituality: A Seeker's Guide* (New York: Random House, 1999), p. 153.

CHAPTER 13

1. Roberts and Amidon, eds., *Honoring the Earth*, n.p.

2. Sharon Gannon and David Life, *Jivamukti Yoga: Practices for Liberating Body and Spirit* (New York: Ballantine Books, 2002), p. 213.

3. Lesser, *The New American Spirituality*, p. 208.

4. Reichard, *Navaho Religion*, p. 288.

5. John Daido Loori, *The Eight Gates of Zen: Spiritual Training in An American Zen Monastery* (Mt. Tremper, N.Y.: Dharma Communications, 1992), p. 246.

6. Loori, p. 243.

7. Phyllis Chesler and Rivka Haut, eds., *Women of the Wall: Claiming Sacred Ground at Judaism's Holy Site* (Woodstock, Vt.: Jewish Lights, 2002).

8. Steven Feld, *Sound and Sentiment: Birds, Weeping, Poetics, and Song in Kaluli Expression* (Philadelphia: University of Pennsylvania Press, 1990).

Further Reading

If our elemental journey whetted your appetite for spiritual discovery, you may want to take a look at this section. Although as a catalog it is more idiosyncratic than comprehensive, the books offered here can be used as stepping stones for your own explorations of religious traditions and the roots of spirituality. Many contain excellent bibliographies that will lead you deeper and deeper. Trust your instincts, be guided by what interests you, and know that you will ultimately find what you need close at hand. Many blessings on your further adventures.

INFORMATIONAL NONFICTION

Armstrong, Karen. *Islam: A Short History*. New York: Modern Library, 2000.
Brooks, Geraldine. *Nine Parts of Desire: The Hidden World of Islamic Women*. New York: Anchor Books, 1996.
Budapest, Z. *The Holy Book of Women's Mysteries, Part II*. Los Angeles: Susan B. Anthony Coven Number One, 1980.
Bulfinch, Thomas. *Bulfinch's Mythology*. New York: Random House, 1993.
Cameron, Julia. *The Artist's Way: A Spiritual Path to Higher Creativity*. New York: Putnam, 1992.
_____. *The Vein of Gold: A Journey to Your Creative Heart*. New York: Jeremy Tarcher/Putnam, 1996.
Campbell, Joseph. *The Power of Myth*. New York: Doubleday, 1988.
Chapple, Christopher Key, and Mary Evelyn Tucker, eds. *Hinduism and Ecology: The Intersection of Earth, Sky, and Water (Religions of the World and Ecology)*. Cambridge, Mass.: Harvard University Press, 2000.

Chesler, Phyllis, and Rivka Haut, eds. *Women of the Wall: Claiming Sacred Ground at Judaism's Holy Site*. Woodstock, Vt.: Jewish Lights, 2002.

Choquette, Sonia. *Your Heart's Desire: Instructions for Creating the Life You Really Want*. New York: Three Rivers, 1997.

Cowan, Tom. *Fire in the Head: Shamanism and the Celtic Spirit*. San Francisco: HarperSanFrancisco, 1993.

———. *Shamanism as a Spiritual Practice for Daily Life*. Freedom, Calif.: Crossing Press, 1996.

———. *The Way of the Saints: Prayers, Practices, and Meditations*. New York: G.P. Putnam's Sons, 1998.

Dening, Sarah. *The Everyday I Ching*. New York: St. Martin's Press, 1995.

Desikachar, T.K.V. *The Heart of Yoga: Developing a Personal Practice*. Rochester, Vt.: Inner Traditions, 1995.

Duerk, Judith. *Circle of Stones*. San Diego: LuraMedia, 1989.

Easwaran, Eknath, trans. *The Bhagavad Gita*. Berkeley: Nilgiri, 1985.

Estés, Clarissa Pinkola. *Women Who Run with the Wolves*. New York: Ballantine, 1992.

Feld, Steven. *Sound and Sentiment: Birds, Weeping, Poetics, and Song in Kaluli Expression*. Philadelphia: University of Pennsylvania Press, 1990.

Fisher, Mary Pat. *Living Religions*. Upper Saddle River, N.J.: Prentice-Hall, 1999.

Frazer, Sir James G. *The Golden Bough: A Study in Magic and Religion*. New York: Macmillan, 1951.

Galland, China. *Longing for Darkness: Tara and the Black Madonna*. New York: Penguin, 1990.

Gannon, Sharon, and David Life. *Jivamukti Yoga: Practices for Liberating Body and Spirit*. New York: Ballantine Books, 2002.

Gimbutas, Marija. *The Language of the Goddess*. San Francisco: HarperSanFrancisco, 1989.

Goldstein, Elyse, ed. *The Woman's Torah Commentary: New Insights from Women Rabbis on the 54 Weekly Torah Portions*. Woodstock, Vt.: Jewish Lights, 2000.

Golinda, Lama Anagarika. *Foundations of Tibetan Mysticism*. New York: Samuel Weiser, 1989.

Halifax, Joan. *Shaman: The Wounded Healer*. London: Thames and Hudson, 1982.

Hill, Julia Butterfly. *The Legacy of Luna: The Story of a Tree, a Woman, and the Struggle to Save the Redwoods.* San Francisco: HarperSanFrancisco, 2001.

———, and Jessica Hurley. *One Makes the Difference: Inspiring Actions That Change Our World.* San Francisco: HarperSanFrancisco, 2002.

Johnson, Cait. *Witch in the Kitchen: Magical Cooking for All Seasons.* Rochester, Vt.: Destiny Books, 2001.

———, and Maura D. Shaw. *Celebrating the Great Mother: A Handbook of Earth-Honoring Activities for Parents and Children.* Rochester, Vt.: Destiny Books, 1995.

Jung, Carl G. *Memories, Dreams, Reflections.* New York: Random House, 1989.

Kamenetz, Rodger. *The Jew in the Lotus: A Poet's Rediscovery of Jewish Identity in Buddhist India.* San Francisco: HarperSanFrancisco, 1995.

Kisshomaru Ueshiba. *The Spirit of Aikido.* New York: Harper and Row, 1987.

LeGuin, Ursula. *Lao Tzu: Tao Te Ching: A Book About the Way and the Power of the Way.* Boston: Shambhala, 1997.

Lesser, Elizabeth. *The New American Spirituality: A Seeker's Guide.* New York: Random House, 1999.

Loori, John Daido. *The Eight Gates of Zen: Spiritual Training in an American Zen Monastery.* Mt. Tremper, N.Y.: Dharma Communications, 1992.

Maguire, Jack. *Waking Up: A Week Inside a Zen Monastery.* Woodstock, Vt.: SkyLight Paths, 2000.

Mascetti, Manuela Dunn, ed. *The Little Book of Zen.* New York: Barnes & Noble Books, 2001.

Matthews, Caitlin. *The Celtic Spirit: Daily Meditations for the Turning Year.* San Francisco: HarperSanFrancisco, 1999.

Merriam-Webster's *Encyclopedia of World Religions.* Springfield, Mass.: Merriam-Webster, Inc., 1999.

Monaghan, Patricia. *The Book of Goddess and Heroines.* St. Paul, Minn.: Llewellyn, 1993.

Montgomery, Pam. *Partner Earth: Restoring Our Sacred Relationship to Nature.* Rochester, Vt.: Destiny Books, 1997.

Moore, Thomas. *Care of the Soul: A Guide for Cultivating Depth and Sacredness in Everyday Life.* New York: HarperCollins, 1992.

Nelson, Marcia Z. *Come and Sit: A Week Inside Meditation Centers.* Woodstock, Vt.: SkyLight Paths, 2001.

Nivedita, Sister, and Ananda K. Coomaraswamy. *Hindus and Buddhists: Myths and Legends.* London: Studio Editions, 1994.

Osbon, Diane K., ed. *Reflections on the Art of Living: A Joseph Campbell Companion.* New York: HarperCollins, 1991.

Porter, Bill. *Road to Heaven: Encounters with Chinese Hermits.* San Francisco: Mercury House, 1993.

Redmond, Layne. *When the Drummers Were Women: A Spiritual History of Rhythm.* New York: Three Rivers Press, 1997.

Reichard, Gladys A. *Navaho Religion.* Princeton: Princeton University Press, 1955.

Rosen, David. *The Tao of Jung.* New York: Penguin, 1996.

Sarangerel. *Chosen by the Spirits: Following Your Shamanic Calling.* Rochester, Vt.: Inner Traditions, 2001.

Sargent, Denny. *Global Ritualism: Myth & Magic Around the World.* St. Paul, Minn.: Llewellyn, 1994.

Scott, Anne. *Serving Fire: Food for Thought, Body, and Soul.* Berkeley: Celestial Arts, 1994.

Starhawk. *The Spiral Dance: A Rebirth of the Ancient Religion of the Great Goddess.* San Francisco: HarperSanFrancisco, 1989.

Stone, Merlin. *Ancient Mirrors of Womanhood.* Boston: Beacon Press, 1990.

Tanahashi, Kazuaki, ed. *Moon in a Dewdrop: Writings of Zen Master Dogen.* New York: Farrar, Straus and Giroux, 1985.

Teish, Luisa. *Jump Up: Good Times Throughout the Seasons with Celebrations from Around the World.* Berkeley: Conari, 2000.

Thurman, Robert A. F. *Inside Tibetan Buddhism: Rituals and Symbols Revealed.* San Francisco: Collins Publishers, 1995.

_____, and Tad Wise. *Circling the Sacred Mountain: A Spiritual Adventure Through the Himalayas.* New York: Bantam, 2000.

Walker, Barbara G. *The Woman's Dictionary of Symbols and Sacred Objects.* San Francisco: HarperSanFrancisco, 1988.

_____. *The Woman's Encyclopedia of Myths and Secrets.* San Francisco: Harper and Row, 1983.

Ward, Tim. *The Great Dragon's Fleas.* Berkeley: Celestial Arts, 1993.

POETRY, PRAYERS, AND FICTION/LITERATURE

Ackerman, Diane. *A Natural History of the Senses.* New York: Random House, 1990.

_____. *Deep Play.* New York: Random House, 1999.

Aizenberg, Susan, and Erin Belieu, eds. *The Extraordinary Tide: New Poetry by American Women*. New York: Columbia University Press, 2001.

Bly, Robert, ed. *The Soul Is Here for Its Own Joy*. Hopewell, N.J.: Ecco Press, 1995.

————, James Hillman, and Michael Meade, eds. *The Rag and Bone Shop of the Heart*. New York: HarperCollins, 1992.

Colette, translated by Enid McLeod. *My Mother's House and Sido*. New York: Farrar, Straus, and Giroux, 1953.

Cunningham, Elizabeth. *Daughter of the Shining Isles*. Barrytown, N.Y.: Station Hill, 2000.

————. *Small Bird: Poems and Prayers*. Barrytown, N.Y.: Station Hill, 2000.

Diamant, Anita. *The Red Tent*. New York: St. Martin's Press, 1997.

Dillard, Annie. *For the Time Being*. New York: Vintage Books, 2000.

Furlong, Monica, ed. *Women Pray: Voices Through the Ages, from Many Faiths, Cultures, and Traditions*. Woodstock, Vt.: SkyLight Paths, 2001.

Linthwaite, Illona, ed. *Ain't I a Woman! A Book of Women's Poetry from Around the World*. New York: Random House, 1993.

Miller, Brenda. *Season of the Body*. Louisville, Ky.: Sarabande, 2002.

Muten, Burleigh, ed. *Her Words: An Anthology of Poetry About the Great Goddess*. Boston: Shambhala, 1999.

————. *Return of the Great Goddess*. Boston: Shambhala, 1994.

Roberts, Elizabeth, and Elias Amidon, eds. *Earth Prayers: From Around the World*. San Francisco: HarperSanFrancisco, 1991.

————. *Honoring the Earth: A Journal of New Earth Prayers*. San Francisco: HarperSanFrancisco, 1997.

Rumi. *The Illuminated Rumi*. Translated by Coleman Barks. New York: Broadway Books, 1997.

Sumrall, Amber Coverdale, and Patrice Vecchione, eds. *Storming Heaven's Gate: An Anthology of Spiritual Writings by Women*. New York: Penguin, 1997.

Tonkinson, Carole, ed. *Big Sky Mind: Buddhism and the Beat Generation*. New York: Riverhead Books, 1995.

Walker, Alice. *The Color Purple*. New York: Simon and Schuster, 1982.

Williams, Terry Tempest. *An Unspoken Hunger*. New York: Random House, 1994.

————. *Red: Passion and Patience in the Desert*. New York: Pantheon Books, 2001.

Printed in the USA
CPSIA information can be obtained
at www.ICGtesting.com
JSHW022332140824
68134JS00019B/1433